THE TURTLE, THE MITTEN,
AND AN EPIC HISTORY OF MICHIGAN

AARON HELMAN

To Erin, who is the real MVP.

CHAPTER ONE
DETROIT

I don't remember how much spaghetti I ate the first time I heard the Ojibwe story of the creation of Michigan, but it was plenty, and it was enough. There had been food and fellowship in the simple log cabin at the top of Greensky Hill, the building itself not more than a single open room filled with the sounds of chatter and laughter, the smell of garlic bread, and the sweat of the humidity that followed us inside. There was salad before the spaghetti and ice cream after, and then, just at the moment when it seemed the evening was about to end, it didn't.

The ceremonial storytellers paraded from an open door at the back of the room, the thumping of their drums announcing their arrival long before we could see them. Tired heads turned on swivels as we wondered what would happen next, and selfishly, how long it would stand between us and sleep. The pounding of the taut deerskin continued until the tribal troubadours turned a rehearsed about-face in front of the picture window that gazed over the Indian burial ground. Suddenly, it was only the whir of a dozen oscillating fans that prevented complete silence from taking hold of the room.

The storytellers invited us to take a seat. There were many places to sit in that church, but I chose the most comfortable one, and that was a mistake. I reclined on the soft chair without meaning to, and while the storytellers exegeted their genesis, I began to fall asleep. I wasn't the only one. Like most of my friends in the room, the day had taken a toll. There were a hundred miles of cycling in my legs and 3,000 calories of carbs in my stomach, and in the middle of all of that, we'd painted the entire exterior of the tribal chapel while dodging angry bees. Wrapped in the warmth of the room, sleep came uninvited and relentless.

It was not a peaceful slumber, interrupted as it was by the punctuations of percussion and occasional tribal whoop. The story came in bits and pieces, recovered and lost again, holes in the narrative filled with vague and slumbering thoughts. It's impossible to remember which parts of the tale I heard and which ones I dreamt, but then maybe that's the point of a story like this one.

As I heard it beneath the heat and humidity of a summer evening in Michigan, there was a great flood, and perhaps it was the same great flood that befell Noah and wiped out his antediluvian contemporaries. Everything solid was lost beneath the waters, including the land that would later become the lower peninsula of the state of Michigan.

As I remember it, there was a council of animals, although I cannot recall where the animals convened given that the wet world left them no place to stand or sit or lay. The animals took turns diving to the bottom of the water to try to retrieve the land, but none of them were able to reach the end of the bottomless sea, each returning with empty hands and burning, gasping lungs.

At last, there was a brave muskrat who offered to make the dive. He was laughed off by the other creatures, but was eventually permitted to make the journey, taking in an enormous breath, and then disappearing into the dark waters for longer than any of the others. By the time he came to the surface, the muskrat was suffocated and dead, but there in his hand was a tiny handful of dirt from the bottom of the sea.

The dirt was spread across the back of a Stoic turtle, where it multiplied and grew and formed the lower peninsula of the state of Michigan. The legend calls Michigan an island in the maritime wild, surrounded on all sides by Great Lakes and also Indiana.

The calm and meditative voice of the storyteller mixed with my exercise-induced somnolence and what was probably just the burning of incense might have proved a hypnosis, because when I slept, I dreamt of the muskrat and the turtle. I saw the other animals, the same ones who had mocked the muskrat in life, and I watched them honor him in his death. I could smell the sweetness of the petals of the fine flowers they laid across his tiny dead body in commemoration of his sacrifice. I watched as they buried him in the very ground that he had retrieved from the depths. I saw them march away from the gravesite and I heard the drums of their parade fade slowly into the distance until I couldn't hear them anymore.

When I woke up, it was morning.

*   *   *

During the next two weeks, I'm accompanying plenty of excellent friends on a bike ride around the entirety of that turtle, tracing the silhouette of a Michigan Mitten that's been emblazoned on hats, shirts, and stickers; then carved into cutting boards, chairbacks, and drink coasters at touristy shops in lake towns up and down both of the state's coasts. That muskrat is far from the last dead animal we'll encounter during the next 1,400 miles and change.

The truth is that the history of Michigan begins wherever you want it to. It could start when the glaciers receded and left behind the massive Great Lakes that define most of its boundaries or when the tribal peoples came from the north and the west to settle a place that – save for the chilly winters – seemed an awful lot like an ideal home. It could start when Europeans visited and settled in the 1620s or when Father Jacque Marquette founded Sault Sainte Marie in 1668. It could start with a turtle and a muskrat and the kind of Gilgametic epic that appears in dozens of other histories and mythologies in cultures all over the world.

But as far as I'm concerned, Michigan, at least as one of the United States of America, begins at some point in the 1670s. That's when a collection of French missionaries crossed Lake St. Clair from Canada and stumbled onto a tribal settlement with an unknown and ancient history. There, the missionaries discovered a stone idol that had been venerated by generations of Native Americans and immediately set to the proper Christian work of destroying the thing with an axe.

The incident may not be Michigan's earliest history, and it may not be its most important history, but it certainly feels like its most American history. It's fitting that the desecration happened in Detroit, always Michigan's most important settlement, and maybe the most American city in the history of the nation.

*   *   *

The first thing I notice in Detroit is the mangy coyote lying dead in exactly the place it shouldn't, its fresh corpse obstructing the right lane of a freeway well within the city's limits. The coyote lies there like an offering to a city that's tired of the sacrifices. The dead dog's eyes would look upon a part of town that is just as dead as it is, except that its eyes don't look at anything anymore, and there's nothing here to see anyway. This is the part of Detroit where the streetlights stopped working a long time ago.

I didn't know that coyotes lived here, and as far as I know, maybe they still don't. I only ever saw one coyote in Detroit, and I saw as much of its insides as I saw anything else. In a dozen other metropolises, a minor tragedy like this one would back up traffic for hours at a time, but in Detroit, there's not enough traffic left to matter. There hasn't been for a while.

This used to be the fifth largest city in America.

Detroit is the dead coyote the same way Detroit is the darkened stone library the same way Detroit is stunning architecture surrounded by broken glass the same way Detroit is prosperity in museums and blight in neighborhoods.

We gawk at the dog's gizzarded remains and we wonder how in the hell *that* happened, but the truth is we already know. We knew before we got here. We just didn't expect the metaphor to be so visceral, but then neither did the driver of the truck who had the misfortune to roadkill a coyote today.

We watch the dead creature stay dead through the car's windows for as long as we can. We don't do anything about it because we don't know what to do and it turns out that no one else knows what to do either.

The next day, an underpaid and understaffed highway department driving a work vehicle that runs on pennies, hope, and Detroit automotive magic will cruise this same stretch of road and pull over long enough to do something about the dead coyote.

They'll set a pair of orange cones on either side of its corpse.

*   *   *

By population and by reputation, Detroit casts a wide shadow over the rest of Michigan, but it is worth noting that Detroit is not Michigan's first settlement, it is not Michigan's capital, and it is not home to either of the state's flagship universities.

And yet, Detroit is undeniably the city that launched its state. It's the city that built America and saved the world *twice*. It's the place that – not that long ago – was the richest city in these United States. Michigan's story starts and ends in Detroit, and even though the nation is loath to admit it, it's the place modern America's story runs through too. We're all waiting to see if it will end here as well.

Three minutes after we see the dead coyote, we hand our car keys over to a bowtied valet and we're ushered into an expired lumber baron's extravagant estate because make no mistake, this is Detroit too, and maybe the truest version of it. For as far as the city's fallen, Detroit has a much longer legacy of wealth than it does poverty. There were titans of industry who planted flags here long before Henry Ford made Americans want to buy cars and build garages. There were fur magnates and lumber monopolists and war profiteers here ever since Detroit spoke French.

That makes the dystopian poverty of modern Detroit an entirely new phenomenon. As recently as the 1950s, Detroit was the richest city in America, and when viewed from the right location and at the right angle, it can still feel that way. There's whiplash in the way a single street can go from poverty to affluence and back again in a matter of blocks, and I am describing all of the streets.

The decline of the great city has been stark enough to seduce a tourism unto itself. Rubberneckers from all over the world have descended like braindead zombies into the city to photograph its downfall and to cosplay their own version of a steampunk apocolaypse staged against the backdrop of shuttered buildings, shattered windows, and occasional crime tapes.

But that's not the story inside the mansion. We slide into a pair of well-polished barstools and order expensive drinks. We're not even a quarter-mile from some from some of the worst parts of the new Detroit, but inside these rich wood walls, we might as well be in a different world, and we're absolutely in a different century. The only way to see out into the modern city from here is through a few million dollars' worth of Tiffany windows crafted with literal rose-colored glass.

The mansion was the brainchild and vanity project of David Whitney Jr., a Massachusetts kid with a proud lineage who wound up in Michigan at a very good time. Of course, in the long history of Detroit, there would be a lot of very good times. All the way back in 1857, Whitney just happened to hit on the first one.

Michigan's first abundant resource was millions of acres of old-growth forest, and Whitney established himself as the premier lumber baron best positioned to expoit them. From his stately office in Detroit, he sold millions of dollars worth of trees he hadn't planted from forests that had grown for centuries and millenia before he ever existed. It may seem like a racket, but it was a racket that was about to shape and reshape the entire nation.

When you hear that Detroit built America, it's a truth that begins long before paved roads and Model T's. Michigan lumber built Chicago before and after the Great Fire. Michigan lumber built Minneapolis, St. Louis, Indianapolis, and Omaha. Most importantly – at least for David Whitney Jr. – it built lumber barons' fortunes and helped Whitney build a very impressive estate.

When the original plans were drawn for the Whitney Mansion, it was to feature 52 rooms, 18 fireplaces, an elevator, and more than 21,000 square feet of residential extravagance. The home was largely built according to plan, at least until Whitney's wife learned that a rival entrepreneur was building a house with 19 fireplaces. Whitney's architect managed to squeeze in another two hearths for his client before constuction was completed in 1894, guaranteeing the home's status as the premiere estate in all of Michigan.

The mansion stands as a relic of an almost impossible opulence. Besides holding more fireplaces than any other residence, the home is covered in elaborate detail works, and, in the trademark style of a lumber baron, the wood here is exquisite. Enormous imported stained glass windows tell the story of the Whitney lineage, but somehow these are the more pedestrian windows of the home. It's said that the original Tiffany glass windows that once looked over the Detroit Athletic Club next door are worth more than everything else in the house combined.

Today it's a restaurant that employs a full-time tour guide. It's the kind of home that reminds you at every turn just how much obscene wealth used to call Detroit home, and if the decorations don't make their point well enough, then the ghosts certainly will, because did I forget to mention that this place is haunted?

Restaurant staff report paranormal occurences in every corner of the estate, especially near windows, in the elevator, and around the carriage house. The mansion has been featured on reality ghost hunting shows on SYFY and the Travel Channel.

It's a curious thing that the ghosts have chosen to settle here when there are so many otherwise unoccupied buildings scattered throughout the city, but then, this one is nicer than most of them. I suppose if I had to choose a location to inhabit for eternity, I'd also select a place that kept a regular supply of high-end bourbon and named its signature beer after me.

Those ghosts and this mansion exist as the last vestiges of the end of Detroit's lumber age, an era that was fading into its twilight even as construction on the Whitney Mansion neared its completion.

The map of Michigan is riddled with towns that failed to survive the end of the 1800s, villages and businesses that were never able to transition from the lumber age into anything else. Some of them crumbled. Some of them very literally sank into the sand.

But Detroit wasn't one of them.

At the turn of the century, as the sun set on the golden age of Michigan lumber, Detroit had a population nearing 300,000 and was the 13th largest city in America. In every possible way, it was going to get much, much bigger.

You *think* you know what happened next in Detroit, but I promise it was bigger and more profound than you could ever imagine. Of course there was Henry Ford, the Ford Motor Company, and the Model T. Then General Motors. Cadillac. Buick. Pontiac. Chrysler. Chevrolet. Hudson. Dodge. Jeep. Geo. Lincoln. Packard. Mercury. Oldsmobile. Plymouth. And no fewer than a hundred other historic car manufacturers.

For a hundred years, Detroit built the cars that built the suburbs and created the market for American summer vacations to Mount Rushmore and Disney World. But then this is just the beginning of the outsized influence that Detroit has had on modern America. They're also the ones who invented the assembly line, phone numbers, and refrigerators. They were the first ones to build concrete roads and the ones who came up with the idea to paint lanes on them.

If there was never a single car that rolled off of Detroit's assembly lines, we'd still have the city to thank – or blame – for many of the most essential hallmarks of current American life. They're the ones who came up with the eight-hour workday, the five-day work week, corporatized pharmaceuticals, and the

9

revolutionary idea that every household should have access to massive quantities of credit and consumer debt.

For 80 years starting in 1903, Detroit was the real center of the United States, even if the proud nation would never admit it. The old saying was that when Detroit came down with a cold, other cities caught pneumonia, and God help us if any part of that sentiment rings true today.

By the middle of the century, Washington was the political capital of the world, New York was the financial capital of the world, Los Angeles was the entertainment capital of the world, and Detroit was the automotive capital of the world. If the average American cared about just one of those things, it was his car. That's why, by 1950, it was Detroit – and not any of those other cities – that was established as the richest city in the richest nation in the world.

It was an honor that was well-deserved and hard-earned. Detroit hadn't just built the fabric of the modern western world, it had also saved it from the brink twice. The first world war was fought in the trenches, but won in the factories of Detroit, where converted automotive plants produced anti-submarine warships and more tactical aircraft than had previously existed in the world.

Twenty years later, when Joe Louis knocked out Max Schmelling at Yankee Stadium in front of 70,000 ravenous fans, it wouldn't be the last time that Detroit punched a Nazi in the mouth.

During World War II, Detroit was the most strategic and protected location in the United States. They stationed a nuke and antiaircraft guns on Belle Isle despite the fact that the midwestern city is more than 500 miles from either coast. The consensus was that, in the event of cataclysmic disaster, the entire Federal government was more replaceable than the Detroit War Machine. Despite the fact that the city was more than 3,000 miles from the nearest battlefield, Detroit nevertheless found itself at the epicenter of another World War.

In the aftermath of armistice, New York and Washington shut down for parades. Chicago and Los Angeles paused for memorials. Philadelphia and Boston gathered the masses for enormous fireworks shows.

And in Detroit? They got back to work, refitting their factories once again for consumer cars instead of tanks, rockets, ships, gun turrets, and helicopters. There was a feeling in the city that the best was yet to come, and the feeling was correct. Detroit was about to reshape western culture in its image all over again, and once again, the American public would never see it coming.

Berry Gordy built the Motown hit machine the same way Ford put out Model T's, running tracks and artists through a musical assembly line in such a way that some of his singers never even met the lyricists, composers, and backing band members that helped make them famous. Along the way, Gordy churned out pop legends one after another: Marvin Gaye, Diana Ross, Stevie Wonder, Smokey Robinson, The Temptations, Gladys Knight, The Jackson 5, and most importantly, The Funk Brothers.

You might not be familiar with that last one, but you've certainly heard them before, and you've heard them a lot. The Funk Brothers were the house band at Motown, a collection of Detroit musicians who recorded instrumentations for every major Motown artist over the course of the 13 years the label made its home in the Motor City. During that short time, The Funk Brothers played on at least 50 number one hits, which is more than Elvis, The Beatles, and Taylor Swift combined.

Motown changed the way musicians were marketed and transformed the way they produced their music. The final test of a

Motown track didn't happen in a sound studio filled with tens of thousands of dollars of the newest technology. Instead, Berry Gordy and his producers would pile into a Chevy Bel Air and play their record through the car's stock speakers. The next time you're out for a long drive, remember that it was Detroit who decided your next road trip should come with a soundtrack.

But Motown wasn't the beginning of Detroit's music scene and it certainly wasn't its end. Long before Martha and the Vandellas were Dancing in the Street, early Detroit was home to the finest concert hall and professional symphony orchestra in the United States. In later years, Miles Davis made it a point to only hire bass players trained in Detroit. Techno music, as a phenomenon and a genre was literally invented here.

There's some point of contention about who the greatest guitar player of all time is, but George Harrison, Keith Richards, and Eric Clapton all bestow that honor upon Detroit guitarist John Lee Hooker. Each cites him as their greatest influence. Even the British invasion sprouted from a seed once planted in Detroit.

The list of Detroit artists who never recorded for Motown might even be more impressive than the list of the ones who did. It's a list that includes Aaliyah, Bob Seger, J Dilla, Sufjan Stevens, Ray Parker, The White Stripes, Big Sean, Alice Cooper, and the Winans family.

It's a list and a history that only becomes more impressive when you realize I haven't yet mentioned Eminem.

Or Madonna.

Or Aretha Franklin.

On Rolling Stone's list of the hundred greatest artists in history, a dozen come from Detroit roots. No other city has more than four. Another list credits Detroit's music scene with the top artist of the 1970s (Stevie Wonder), the top two artists of the 1980s (Madonna and Michael Jackson), the top artist of the 2000s (Eminem), and the greatest singer of all time (Franklin).

It would be easy to say that Detroit sits atop the popular music throne, but in fact, it sits upon many of them. In all, the Detroit music machine has helped to coronate the Princess of R&B, the Godfather of Shock Rock, the Empress of Soul, the Queen of Soul, the Prince of Soul, the First Family of Soul, the King of Pop, the Queen of Pop, a Godfather of Punk, the King of Motown, the Godfathers of Techno, a Rap God, the King of the Grammys, and whatever the hell Kid Rock is.[1]

Virtually every part of your morning commute is brought to you by Detroit, from the car you drive to the road you drive on to the tunes you play on the trip. The playlist of Detroit music that I listened to while prepping this chapter lasted more than five-and-a-half hours and that was just the songs that hit number one.

We spent a full Saturday in Detroit before we prepared to tackle the Turtle and we packed as much into it as we could. We trekked to Belle Isle, once known as the Paris of the Midwest. We strolled the DIA. We visited Motown and toured the Ford Museum. We ate square pizza and chased the pizza with a Vernor's float. We didn't do all the Detroit things, but we got pretty close, and come Sunday morning, we're going to do the most Detroit thing of all.

We're going to leave.

Today's Detroit has a population of about 600,000 people, fewer than a third of its peak population in 1950. In just seventy years, Detroit lost from its city limits the entire population of Dallas.

---

[1] In order: Aaliyah, Alice Cooper, Gladys Knight, Aretha Franklin, Mavin Gaye, The Jackson 5, Michael Jackson, Madonna, Iggy Pop, Smokey Robinson, The Belleville Three, Eminem, Stevie Wonder, and whatever the hell Kid Rock is.

The city is stretched beyond its limits, left to care for a deteriorating infrastructure that was designed to accommodate two million people, but with a current tax base that's barely a quarter of that. It's no wonder the coyotes get left behind. There are nearly 100,000 vacant buildings within the city limits. Left without options and largely without hope, Detroit declared bankruptcy in July 2013.

It took just 50 years for the richest city in America to go broke.

As we sit at the polished bartop on the third floor of the Whitney Mansion, we have the luxury to sit like royalty and pretend that none of it ever happened, or at least like none of it has happened yet. The bartender asks me if I want another drink, and given the soaring Michigan temperatures and the 94 miles of cycling built into tomorrow's route, I should say no, but I don't.

There will come a reckoning for me on the streets of Detroit tomorrow, but then, there's been a reckoning on the streets of Detroit for everyone, every day, for the past forty years.

CHAPTER TWO
EXODUS

As we approach the southernmost extreme of Detroit's city limits, it's not hard to understand why that kid from that Journey song was so eager to take the midnight train going literally anywhere else. By the looks of things, it might have been a full train.

In this part of the city, there is almost no one left.

It's been four miles of stop-and-start cycling, and we're already well into exactly the kind of abandoned urban dystopia that you probably imagine when you imagine modern Detroit. There are crumbling brick buildings, overgrown parking lots, entire trees sprouting through cracks in disused concretes. Every window is shattered. There is nothing left for the scrappers to rescue. Something is on fire because out here there is always something on fire, and more importantly, there is no one to extinguish it.

Of course, despite what Steve Perry's anthemic warblings might claim, true Detroiters know there's no such place as South Detroit. Detroit's city center is built directly on the edge of the Detroit River – and on the edge of the United States. If there's such a place as South Detroit, it's more properly called Windsor and it's in Canada.

But there is a southwestern part of Detroit and that's where we are now. I am immensely glad not to be here alone. Somehow, I've persuaded my wife to join me, because what could be better use of her limited vacation time than a scenic cycling tour of District 12? We've also convinced our friend Andrew to come along, and somewhere out there, his wife Erin is driving our support vehicle, navigating a phalanx of orange barrels.

This would be more road construction than any of us have ever seen, at least until we learned that there was never any construction, and in many cases, there were no roads. Without the funds to repair its shattered streets, Detroit has been left no choice but to offline entire sections of the grid. Out here, these roads aren't closed for repair. They're closed for good.

This is Delray, described to me by one person as the Detroit of Detroit. Delray is abandoned, crumbling, burning, and broken. Delray is a fiduciary black hole for the city's accountants. It's a headache for politicians, an eyesore for commuters, a blighted wasteland for gawking tourists.

And for a handful of people, it's home.

*   *   *

Delray has always given people myriad reasons to leave, and in the face of those reasons, some number of gritty Detroiters have always stayed anyway. A hundred years ago, the people of Delray were left to choke and wheeze on the most polluted air in the city. They tied rags around their faces and they stayed. When the factories and plants moved in even closer and the people were surrounded by the stereophonic sounds of Detroit's peak noise pollution, they stuffed cotton swabs in their ears, but did not leave their homes. And in the 1930s, when their tiny, sooted, urban hamlet became domain of The Witch, they did not run, not even from her.

During the second half of the 1920s, a Hungarian immigrant named Rose Veres opened a boarding house in Delray, hosting men who were down on their luck, new to town, or just tired of sleeping beneath bridges. Hers was an attractive spot due to its friendly terms, requiring very little money down to secure a room. A bed and a shower could be had at the house for not more than the low price of a signed life insurance policy payable to Rose Veres in the event of the guest's untimely death. For the men who stayed in her home, those untimely deaths were uncommonly common. By the time the twelfth man turned up dead in her home, Veres had earned her nickname. They called her the Witch of Delray, and she'd managed to collect insurance payouts on all twelve of them.

In 1931, the Witch was taken to trial, found guilty of murder and sentenced to life in prison along with her son. She loudly protested her innocence, maintaining that she was neither a murderer nor a witch. Of course, that didn't jive well with the thing that happened next.

By legend or by quote, Veres placed a centurylong hex on the people of Delray, and by all appearances, it must have been a potent one. Veres was somehow exonerated of her sentence and released after a 1945 retrial, but a quick bike ride through what's left of Delray indicates that she did not revoke the curse.

For those less inclined to believe in the occult, there's plenty of evidence that the curse was already there, long before the Witch of Delray thought to issue it. Delray's position within Detroit gave it a kind of Stockholm Syndrome relationship with the larger city. Its economy absolutely relied on the continued expansion of manufacturing efforts, even as those expansions decimated the quality of life in the neighborhood.

Unchecked and unregulated growth sent cancer and birth defect rates skyrocketing in Delray even as life expectancy plummeted. But when that growth slowed, Delray was visited by evictions, homelessness, and starvation.

Caught between a rock a hard place and sidled by economic devastation, governmental red tape, and the occasional corrupt policymaker, you don't even need the trope of a witch's curse to explain everything that happened next.

But it doesn't hurt.

If Rose Veres really did put a hundred-year curse on this place, then it was certainly a doozy. First came the freefall of the automotive industry, shuttering plants and the hundreds of other ancillary businesses that supported them. It was too late now, of course, to somehow undo all of the environmental damage; and by the 1980s, Delray was a polluted and decripit neighborhood that had been robbed of its jobs. Given no choice, a lot of people left.

But not all of them.

Human beings hold a strange sentimentality for the concept of home. For the past five decades, hangers-on have remained in Delray, without reason and without hope. Every year a few more people die and a few more than that finally give up. Delray is dying, but so far, it's been a very slow death.

It's insensitive, but not inaccurate, to point out that Delray is a burden on greater Detroit. As long as people continue to live there, Detroit's taxpayers are on the hook to make sure that basic infrastructure remains in place. Water has to run, electricity has to flow, sewage has to be removed, streetlights have to stay on, and at least some of the roads have to remain navigable.

Until recently, eminent domain was not an option at Detroit's disposal to move people from their homes. The government can only forcibly seize property in order to develop something for the public good, but Detroit didn't want to *develop* anything here. They wanted to abandon it. Occasional efforts to buy out residents were stymied by legal red tape that prevented the city from offering more for property than it was appraised for. Since the homes were mostly worthless, the only cash payouts they could

18

offer were insultingly low, certainly not enough for homeowners to uproot their lives and find a decent place elsewhere. For many, Delray was far from ideal, but it was at least a roof over their heads. They knew plenty of people who didn't even have that much.

Detroit may not have had the tools at their disposal to incentivize the last remnants of Delray to move, but they had another set of tools at their disposal. They could find ways to disincentivize people from staying. They solicited a glue factory to set up shop just on the outskirts of the neighborhood. One woman said they were trying to *stink her out*. Another called it a *deliberate municipal poisoning*. Both stayed.

I talked with people who are certain that police patrols have been reduced, that the town is intentionally refusing to send the street sweeper their way, and one woman who is sure that Detroit is sending all of its extra heat into Delray. I was not able to get her to explain exactly how they are able to do that. She intends to stay.

In 2013, Delray was announced as the site of the Gordie Howe International bridge, a massive undertaking that will provide Detroit's third connection to Canada. Besides the boon the span promises to create, the project came with the added benefit of finally allowing the city to seize properties throughout Delray, displacing hundreds of homeowners by forcible and legal means, while making it that much worse for the ones left behind.

A roughly plotted trendline of the neighborhood's declining population shows it hitting zero in 2031, exactly a hundred years after the Witch of Delray offered her curse.

*   *   *

Delray is not a great place to ride a bicycle. The roads are quiet enough, but they're covered with garbage and detritus. The scenery is not awesome, and as for the smell of Delray that so many complain about, it's real. The shuttered buildings are visibly crumbling, and for that matter, so are the open ones. We cruise beneath the skeleton of the Gordie Howe Bridge, no doubt an impressive engineering feat, but for so many people, just another way to get the hell out of Detroit as fast as possible.

Abandonment is kind of a theme here, and it's not a modern theme either. During the War of 1812, a force of British troops and their tribal allies surrounded Detroit, and despite the fact that the Americans had their aggressors outnumbered almost 2-to-1, they surrendered the city *without a fight*. Detroit remains the only American city to ever be surrendered to a foreign country.

When General William Hull waved a white tablecloth toward his enemies and surrendered more than 2,000 men, thousands of guns, the only armed American vessel in the region, and more than $200,000 of booty; it wasn't the last time that the nation would turn its back on Detroit. Hull carried the shame of that surrender for the rest of his life, faced a livid court-martial, and remains the only American general sentenced to death for cowardice. His life was only saved when President James Madison personally stayed the execution.

Ever since then, it's been one kick in the gut after another. More than fifty automotive companies have shut down and left town since 1920. Motown left for California in 1972. Vernor's was acquired in 1985 and bottling operations moved to the other side of the state. Stroh's left in 1999. And on a Sunday in 2024; as we crossed over the Rouge River on the Jefferson Avenue Bridge, we left Detroit too.

The road begins to deindustrialize by degrees as we pedal beyond the city, but we are not into the country, and these are not the suburbs either. The town of River Rouge functions as an extension of Detroit in form and feel. Like its big brother to the north, River Rouge has shed two-thirds of its population in the past fifty years; and just like Detroit, it's leaning hard on a smaller and less affluent tax base to maintain the infrastructure of a town that's much bigger than it needs to be anymore. It's the same blight, but on a different scale. Abandoned strip malls replace dwindling city blocks and there's a little more green space between the crumbling buildings. Who knows? Maybe that does count for a suburb in this part of the country.

*   *   *

It's seven miles before we begin to escape from beneath the shadow of the Detroit automobile machine. Which isn't to say that it *feels* any different, but at least the history of this newest wave of dystopia has a different flavor to it.

The city of Ecorse used to be known as America's *Little Venice* and was once home to the Great Lakes Engineering Works, the most powerful shipbuilding operation on all of the Great Lakes. This is where the Edmund Fitzgerald came from, and it will take longer for Gordon Lightfoot to sing about that famous boat than it will for us to cycle through what's left of the city it came from.

It turns out that the market for American steamships cratered even before the market for American cars. By 1960, the Engineering Works was sold off and stripped for parts. Ecorse was left reeling and just like their most famous boat, they'd hit rock bottom just a few years later. Ecorse was the first city in Michigan to declare bankruptcy in 1986.

As for the town, it turns out that boat-related municipal hardships look a lot like car-related ones. Ecorse looks a lot like the other places we've seen – broken, empty, and struggling for hope. It has not yet emerged from its 1986 bankruptcy. The state declared a financial emergency for Ecorse in 2009; then arrested its mayor and city controller on charges of conspiracy, bribery, and fraud shortly thereafter. It seems like it's a far cry from the heyday of the city, but then, maybe not. That's because the biggest boom this town ever saw came with plenty of racketeering.

During Prohibition winters, rumrunners used to deliver their contraband liquors across the frozen Detroit River from Canada. Their destination was a section of Ecorse called Hogan's Alley, where wealthy bootleggers and gangsters covered themselvs in fancy clothes, gaudy diamonds, and extravagant watches. There was good money in boatbuilding, but there was better money in smuggling. For a while, it was the most dangerous place in America for teetotaling Feds and even spawned the only ice skating pirate I've ever heard of. The Grey Ghost was never caught and never identified, but he robbed and plundered hundreds of runners and pullers during the frosty Michigan winters, snagging them on the way back to Canada and relieving them of their cash.

A hundred years later, the river doesn't freeze so often anymore and there are a lot less diamonds worn by the men in the clubs, but from the looks of the gutters on the sides of the road, there's still more than enough alcohol to go around. According to the locals, it seems that plundering is still a problem.

We've been riding bikes for half-an-hour. We haven't seen The Grey Ghost just yet, but there's still a very long way to go.

22

CHAPTER THREE
THE VICTORS WRITE THE HISTORY

During the decades before Thomas Jefferson and the Americans declared their independence, the English and the French were engaged in the planet's first World War, 150 years before they had a name for such a thing. The Seven Years' War gets forgotten mostly because its name makes it sound like a triviality, but it was the first truly global conflict, and it killed more than a million people in battles across Europe, Asia, and North America.

The war even had a Michigan theater, and we're cycling right through the middle of it, stopped at a park outside of Ecorse while Little Leaguers hone their skills on the diamond behind us. This is Council Point, and 260 years before we rolled into it, Chief Pontiac of the Ottawa Tribe used it to raise an army.

Pontiac gathered leaders from Michigan's Potawatomi and Wyandot tribes and urged them to fight back against the British who had taken Detroit from the French. The prevailing thought was that things had been better under the French, although it's not known if there was much truth to that. At best, the French were only *slightly* less exploitative than the British invaders. But for the Native Americans, perhaps the French were the devil they knew, and when the devil called in a favor, Pontiac was eager to oblige. In fiction or in truth, he told the gathered chiefs that they had a promise of friendship waiting for them from the King of France if they could drive the Brits from Fort Detroit. There's no hard proof that such a promise existed and even less that the French were inclined to keep to their half of the deal if it did.

The truth is that the exploitation of Native Americans across Michigan arrived in many different forms. They were ripped off in trading deals and driven from their ancestral lands. They were used as collateral in conflicts that were not their own. In this one, all the best scholarship suggests that Pontiac was a pawn and not a partner, but that's not the story that's most often told.

According to the unsubstantiated annals of history, Pontiac gathered the tribal chiefs beneath a tree not far from the picnic table we stopped at on our bike ride. There, he launched into an extemporaneous speech that called their British overlords "proud, imperious, churlish, and haughty."

But if the apocrypha is to be believed, Pontiac saved his best words to praise the French who had once ruled over the land with kindness and benevolence. It's a speech that conveniently forgets that these were the same ones who forced the natives from their land in the first place, that it was the French missionaries who originated the desecration of their sacred idols and their holy lands. It's also a speech that almost certainly never happened:

"The French familiarized themselves with us, studied our tongue and manners, wore our dress, married our daughters, and our sons their maids, dealt honestly, and well supplied our wants, used no one ill, and treated with respect our kings, our captains, and our aged men; called us their friends, nay, what is more, their children. And seemed like fathers anxious for our welfare."

It's a wild, Francophilian discourse that borders on the unbelievable, and frankly, should not be believed. Did the brave and daring Chief Pontiac really gather the most powerful leaders of the most powerful Michigan tribes to launch a war with a rah-rah speech that called the French their daddies?

Probably not. But the chronicler who attributes him the quote was a Frenchman, and it's the victors who write the history.

24

Whatever he said at Council Point, Pontiac was able to forge a military alliance between Michigan's dominant tribes – the Ottawa, Potawatomi, and Wyandot. A few weeks later, more than a thousand Native American troops set upon Fort Detroit and laid siege to it for six months.

Despite several ancillary victories, Pontiac's forces were never able to take the fort and were never able to test the veracity of the French king's promise. Six months after the siege began, it ended, and Pontiac was driven out of Michigan. So too were the French, forced in the terms of their surrender to cede all North American land east of the Mississippi to the Brits.

Pontiac would not quit. Even without the support of his French fathers, he would continue to provoke the churlish Brits until his assassination in 1769.

For the three of us on our bikes, we're following Pontiac's retreat south through Wyandotte, the town named after a full third of his fighting force and one of three dominant tribes that made up this part of Michigan. Wyandotte is still shaded by the looming shadow of Detroit, and like every other place we've been so far, there's still a struggle to recover from a population that's cratered in the past fifty years.

But there's also evidence that Wyandotte has turned a corner. The blight is less visceral here, or else it's been pushed off to roads that we haven't seen. The charming downtown is filled with gastropubs, art galleries, boutiques, and cafes; but with just enough Detroit grit to keep it from feeling too idyllic.

I desperately try to convince the crew to stop for a drink at Bobcat Bonnie's, but they point out that there's still 53 miles of cycling left in today's route and that it's also not yet noon. We keep riding some three-and-a-half miles through Wyandotte down Biddle

Avenue, a road that honors an honorable man, but one who hasn't quite earned *all* of the accolades given him.

John Biddle came from prestigious Philadelphia stock, was educated at Princeton, and served with distinction beneath Winfield Scott during the War of 1812. He was later elected the fourth Mayor of Detroit and spent a term as the Michigan Territory's non-voting delegate to the U.S. House of Representatives. He served as speaker in the Michigan House of Representatives and was named president of the Michigan Central Railroad.

Any of these would have been fine reasons to name a street after Mr. Biddle, but none of them are the reason that was chosen. Instead, Biddle Avenue cuts a vertical line through Wyandotte because its namesake is recognized as being the area's first settler.

He wasn't.

The French had been in the region for more than a century before Biddle arrived on the scene, and enough generations of Wyandot Indians lived in the territory before that for Biddle to literally name the town after them. But it's the victors who write the history, and so when Lucille Ball moved here with her parents, she got to live on the historic Biddle Avenue, and we got to pass the spot where her home used to stand on the way out of town.

As for those first peoples, the Wyandot ceded their land to the Americans at the Treaty of Detroit in 1807. They were relocated to Kansas in the 1840s, then relocated again to Oklahoma in the aftermath of the Civil War. Their numbers have been decimated in the centuries and decades since. Despite the city's own population decline, there are still more people living in Wyandotte than there are Wyandot people remaining.

The history of the Wyandot is one that's been squashed a little bit and probably not by accident. Forty years after they joined

Pontiac's Rebellion against the British, they found themselves in an unlikely alliance with their former enemies, striking a peace with the Throne in order to defy the expansion hungry Americans. The Brits had become the known devil, less exploitative by degrees, and anyway, in this chess match, they're the ones that held the pawns.

The British must have studied their own military history, because they seized on a familiar strategy that had once been used against them. Like the French had once done with Pontiac, the Brits solicited a charismatic tribal leader named Tecumseh, made him a promise of friendship, and made him their mouthpiece to raise up a Native American army.

The Native Americans had every reason to distrust the Brits, and tensions between the tenuous allies were never fully smoothed. But an unbelievable promise of friendship was better than a very believable promise of belligerence, and that's what the Americans had offered.

Tecumseh picked up where Pontiac left off, uniting local tribes with a former enemy to take on an unknown foe. Their first major operation would be the second Siege of Detroit in fifty years. Pontiac had sought to drive the Brits out. Now Tecumseh endeavored to put them back in.

It's tough to determine exactly *when* a war begins, but if you count it from its first battle, then the War of 1812 began when Tecumseh's men launched into the Battle of Monguagon on August 9 of that same year. It's not where the first shot of the war was fired, and it's not where the first of the violence was exchanged, but it was the first conflict large enough to be called a full-on battle.

We ride through Trenton, Michigan, past the places where muskets were discharged at Native Americans. We see what remains of the thick woods where ambushing forces would have pounced

27

upon their unsuspecting victims. We imagine moments of chaos and calamity. We pilot our bikes across open spaces where 24 people died, six of them Native Americans placed into the service of a king they didn't know and for a cause they couldn't annunciate.

All they knew was that they needed to destroy or delay a northbound American force marching to resupply Fort Detroit. Unfortunately for Tecumseh, he did not realize that his troops were outnumbered 3-to-1. Unfortunately for the Americans, they also did not realize they outnumbered their foes 3-to-1.

A confusing haze of war descended on men who were perhaps not ready for it, and things devolved in a hurry. Tecumseh's troops engaged in more friendly fire than the chief would have liked, and somehow the Americans suffered heavier losses than their outgunned foes – even though those outgunned foes spent a good chunk of the battle *shooting each other.*

The aggressions ended with a British-Indian retreat that the Americans did not trust, and the resupply stalled for several days while the spooked patriots wondered how many more forces were hidden in the woods ahead. There weren't any.

The Americans were quick to claim victory in the Battle of Monguagon, but the conflict achieved Tecumseh's purpose, delaying the resupply long enough for the British and Native American alliance to capture Detroit a week later. Tecumseh succeeded where Pontiac had not. Under the terms of surrender, the Americans were forced to hand over every item in the resupply train that never even made it to the city in the first place.

It was the high moment of Tecumseh's War, and it was not to last. A year later, Tecumseh was killed on the Canadian side of the Detroit River, a blow that led to the dissolution of his tribal confederacy. The Brits would be booted from the continent altogether a year after that. The Americans won the victory, and it's the victors who write the history. That's probably why the historical marker on the side of the road in Trenton remembers the bloody and catastrophic disruption of the American supply train as a specifically *American* victory – the only one in the Michigan theater of the War of 1812.

*   *   *

We ride south through Gibraltar and watch the Detroit River spill unceremoniously into Lake Erie and it all just looks like water from the shore. We navigate inland toward Rockwood, and it's not until we cross the Huron River that the tenor and terrain of the ride begins to change. It's been 21 miles, 29 pages, and two-and-a-half chapters, but we're finally out of Wayne County.

It's another world out here and it happens almost immediately. For the first time on this course, we ride through parts of the landscape where it is possible to not see a building – condemned, occupied, or otherwise – for whole minutes at a time. The roads are quiet in a serene way instead of a dystopian one. The air is fresh. On some occasions, Michigan's neat, paved roads give way to fresh-rocked gravel. Some of the accoutrements of the country are better than others.

We pass a sheep farm, a family cemetery, an Amish father commanding his carriage with a steady hand and a mature beard. There's an unscheduled wildness to Michigan farmlands that you don't find in Indiana and Ohio. There are more trees here. The roads follow the fields; they don't carve them. In Michigan, it's not impossible to imagine the way things used to be.

For as much as Michigan has become synonymous with unchecked industrialization, more than half of the state is still covered in woodlands. Another quarter is agricultural. It's the part we love to ride through and the part that Tim Allen tried to tell you about in those Pure Michigan commercials.

Most importantly, this is where the chicken statues are.

See, my friends and I do a weird thing on bike rides.

We look for chicken statues. We're not sure how it started and we're less sure how it continued, but no matter where we go, we always break up the monotony of long rides by enthusiastically calling out the chicken statues that we see in people's yards as we pass by. There are more of them than you would think.

There is a particularly impressive one on an unpaved road somewhere north of Newport. I know this because I dismounted my bike long enough to snap a photo of the glorious thing before being chased off by its irate owner. The man did not believe me when I told him I was a cycling historian who also catalogued rural chicken statues, which I realize now is a fairly unbelievable explanation to offer.

Anyway, the man set to chase me down in a golf cart and I dashed off down the silliest backwoods Michigan racetrack I've ever been a part of. I caught up to Andrew and Ashley and we made our escape. The man did not catch us.

*   *   *

Ten miles and two more chicken statues later, we're into Monroe, eating granola bars at another battlefield. This one is the goriest and most awful, remembering the deadliest day in the history of Michigan and the bloodiest American days in the War of 1812.

30

The River Raisin National Battlefield Park is an unexpected memorial in an unexpected place. There are only four such parks in the United States, two in Virginia, one in Georgia, and one in Monroe, Michigan, which also happens to be the birthplace of Christie Brinkley.

Six months after Tecumseh's successful siege of Detroit, American forces were still unable to take it back, but they were trying. A detachment of Kentucky militia had marched across Ohio and all the way to the River Raisin under the command of Lieutenant Colonel William Lewis. Finding the river frozen and navigable, his forces pushed to liberate Frenchtown, located at what is now Monroe. They imagined using Frenchtown as a staging ground for their future attempts to retake Detroit.

Frenchtown appeared ripe for the taking and the fight went down as quickly and easily as any military battle can be expected to go. A dozen men were killed, scores more were injured, but in the length of an afternoon; the Americans had seized Frenchtown and driven the Brits and the Indians away.

Four days later, the Brits and the Natives were back with a vengeance and with a fighting force that would guarantee a different result. The early morning attack came as a surprise to the sleepy Americans, and the bulk of the conflict lasted just twenty minutes. When the brief dust settled, nearly 400 Americans were killed and another 500 were taken prisoner unconditionally. Many of those prisoners were killed while being marched toward their internment camps if they were unable or unwilling to keep up. The ones who were laid up in sick beds were killed before they could even attempt the journey.

The Battle of the River Raisin quickly turned into the River Raisin Massacre as a historic fact and a media phenomenon. It represented a level of savagery and violence that was not new to war but was not the kind of thing that was supposed to happen to the Americans, and especially not on their own turf. Twenty years before there was ever a need to remember the Alamo, there was the Raisin, a point of national sorrow, pride, and unity.

When Kentucky newspapers ran headlines to "Remember the Raisin!", men dashed off to enlist to fight in record numbers. Eight of Kentucky's counties are named after men who died in the massacre. Monroe's Kentucky Avenue remembers the militiamen who died there and unites Michigan and Kentucky in something else besides just hating Indiana.

The River Raisin Massacre is an episode that is notable for its enormous cost in human life, its macabre grip on the American psyche, and as another American embarrassment in the Michigan theater of the War of 1812.

But it's an episode that should have never happened.

Brigadier General James Winchester had orders to wait some 30 miles south of the River Raisin. He was never supposed to send Lewis and the Kentucky militia to check out Frenchtown, and when Lewis and his men arrived there, they were never supposed to attack it. Not yet anyway.

By the time Winchester arrived to find that his men had cleared Frenchtown, he should have realized that a counterattack was imminent. He should have realized that his men didn't have enough ammunition to hold their ground in case of an invasion. He didn't, and he didn't.

He should have bothered to lock the doors or post sentries. He didn't do that either. Convinced that the Brits would take weeks to recover from their whipping, he and his men made themselves comfortable in Frenchtown while they waited for armed and experienced reinforcements to show up and offer their congratulations. The reinforcements were still days away when the first musket shots hit. It would be another eight months before the Americans took back Detroit and three more weeks after that before they reclaimed Frenchtown. Besides the immense death toll of the Battle of the River Raisin, it was a failure that would stretch the war out for at least another half-a-year, leading to hundreds more deaths on battlefields across the continent.

The cry to *Remember the Raisin!* should have been a warning to brash and hotheaded militarists, a hard-learned lesson about charging into tactical victories at the expense of strategic defeats. But it became none of those things. It became a rallying cry against the savagery and brutishness of their enemies. After all, it's the victors who write the history.

As for Monroe, it's a town that carries plenty of reminders of the scars it suffered at the hands of the Native Americans. The River Raisin National Battlefield Park is just the beginning, and this isn't even the most *famous* massacre that's remembered here. After all, this town is the home of George Custer, and his statue is less than a mile away.

It's hard to believe now, given the horrible and infamous way General Custer's life ended, but once upon a time, it was considered a boon to be kissed by *Custer's Luck*. And right up until the very end, that's what they called it when a soldier had the regular good fortune to be in the right place at the right time.

For Custer, that first right place was in Monroe, living with a relative so that he could get the education he would need in order to become the folk hero he would become. But Custer might not have valued that education as much as he should have. He earned an early reputation as a practical joker and needed more luck than wits to graduate through West Point. But then, he always had luck.

Custer's performance as a cadet was less than sterling. He graduated last in his class and racked up a record number of demerits during his years in the military academy. Under normal circumstances, he might not have been allowed to see his studies through to the finish, but the years before the Civil War were not normal times. His cohort at West Point had been decimated by abandonments from haughty Confederates eager to go back to the south. With war looming, the military cut a year off of the matriculation path for Custer and his remaining peers. Desperate for officers, they pushed each one of them through to graduation.

Getting out of school early would turn out to be an undeniably lucky break for newly minted Brigadier General George Custer. His first command would have him overseeing the Michigan Brigade, and his first marching orders would send him directly to a battle at Gettysburg, or more correctly, The Battle of Gettysburg.

Just 23 years old, Custer would immediately earn his reputation as a daring, bold commander. His actions on the battlefield were equal parts brilliant, gutsy, and reckless. George Custer was a major reason the Union won that pivotal conflict, but at the same time, his brigade suffered more losses on the field than any other on his side of the battle. This last part wouldn't stick with him as much, because it's the victors who write the history.

Custer's luck would see him arrive just in time to bask in the glow of victory at Waynesboro. He was in the right place at the right time when the Confederates moved to surrender, accepting the first white flag from the enemy and standing present in the room at Appomattox Court House a few days later when General Lee made everything official.

He hadn't always played the most significant role in every conflict, but he'd always been there, the Boy General with the preternatural sense to show up on time. The newspapers loved him, and by the time the war ended, Monroe's own George Custer was among the three or four most celebrated military figures in the nation. Custer's Luck had become a *thing*.

Custer tried his hand at a few things during the next few years, but he was a man who needed to be at war, and so that's exactly where he ended up in the end. His braggadocio led him into a conflict with President Ulysses S. Grant that came to a head when Grant had Custer briefly arrested in Chicago. It might have seemed like a spot of rare bad luck for the Boy General, but only George Custer could turn a setback like that into a boon. In the aftermath of the arrest, newspapers lambasted Grant, calling him a "modern day Caesar", and bandying that Custer ought to take Grant's seat in the White House. Custer took command of his men once again, intent to show more military heroics to the people of his country and maybe earn his way into a next life as their President.

Of course, luck has a tendency to run out. Custer's did, anyway. In south Montana in the summer of 1876, for the first time in his life, General George Custer found himself in the wrong place at the wrong time. Outnumbered as much as ten-to-one by a group of Native Americans who were plainly defending their own land, Custer and his troops were cut down and obliterated. People stopped referring to Custer's Luck as an idiom almost immediately afterward.

For the Lakota and Cheyenne warriors who won the day, it would prove to be a short-lived victory. The truth of the matter is that it was the Americans who were the aggressors in that conflict. The truth is that Custer had been charged to lead a militia into land that wasn't theirs in order to drive the rightful residents from their homes so that white people could get more gold. But the truth doesn't matter when the victors write the history.

After the brutal massacre of one of the nation's most beloved Civil War heroes, the nation's resolve steeled toward the Native Americans. They redoubled their efforts, their troops, and their funding. Within a year, the war would be made over, the land would be taken, and as punishment for their perceived aggression, the Native Americans would receive no recompense for the acreage.

The George Custer statue in Monroe does not depict his moments at the Battle of Little Bighorn. It does not portray him as particularly daring or brave. It's a curious thing. The Custer atop that horse at Elm and Monroe Streets is not in the middle of a charge. His horse has its head down, and Custer's arms are calm at his side, a statuesque still life of a man who never lived one.

Of course, none of this is to denigrate George Custer, a complicated hero in a nation that is full of them. But his life and his luck are undeniably colored by the fact that he was always on the winning side of the wars even when he wasn't on the winning side of the battle. The First Nations people would have a different story to tell about George Custer; just like they'd have a different story to tell about James Winchester, William Lewis, and John Biddle; just like they'd have a different story to tell about the Americans and the British before them and the French before them.

But too often, their story doesn't get heard. A popular refrain buries the Native Americans whenever a historian launches into a history of Michigan, a tacit preface that assumes everything and tells nothing. It goes without saying that the Europeans weren't the first ones to arrive here, someone will explain, and maybe that's exactly the problem.

CHAPTER FOUR
TOLEDO

Fifteen miles south of Monroe; Ashley, Andrew, and I find ourselves flirting with Michigan's southern boundary, the kind of state line that would be invisible and indistinguishable in other places, but up here, it might as well be painted across the road in maize and blue. Our route plays that line like a slalom course, bouncing back and forth between two states, jumping from one distinct midwestern landscape to another. We watch the changes happening without meaning to.

We can't miss it.

See northern Ohio, each of its roads part of a graph paper grid, unshaded by trees, every farmer's field planted in uniform and militaristic rows, each plot planned and designed and delivered on schedule. As for the cycling, it's not that there's more wind in Ohio, it's just that there aren't any trees to block it.

At least until the route turns and bends back into Michigan. The wind hides behind the trees or maybe we do. We see a deer almost immediately and she is the one more surprised by the encounter. There is a couch in the overgrowth covered with empty beer cans and the other rural detritus of a mosquito-bitten night of underage revelry.

Birds chirp and sing above the places where the land has become feral, native plants and weeds reclaiming a land that was never fully taken away from them in the first place. We jog a half-a-mile back and forth from an Ohio that insists on order and into a Michigan that bristles against it. There used to be an old wives' tale that the ticks who carried Lyme disease never advanced south beyond the state line, and the rumor isn't true, but the transforming landscape is enough to almost make you believe it.

Across again to an Ohio where cars are stacked neatly into driveways and then to a Michigan where they're strewn about the occasional unmowed yard. It's not the Yukon up here and it's not even the Upper Peninsula, but there's something delightfully wild about every inch of this state. When we cross into Toledo for good, it all disappears, replaced instead by an Ohioan organization and order that never should have been here. This isn't Michigan anymore. That much is obvious, and we don't need the signs at the line to tell us.

But it's not the way it was supposed to be.

By rule and by right, Toledo should still be in Michigan, and as we lay our heads down for a well-deserved sleep in this Toledo hotel, so should we. There's another bike ride to come in the morning, and it's worth the journey just to figure out how this controversial state line happened and to remember the forgotten civil war that almost was.

*　　*　　*

In the early days of the nation, official boundaries were defined by legally binding written descriptions based on rough and often inaccurate maps. In the case of the Michigan Territory, its southern terminus was written to be an east-west line drawn through the southern tip of Lake Michigan. It's a pretty straightforward description, except that when Ohio became a state in 1803, no one had fully surveyed Lake Michigan to determine exactly where its southernmost point was.

The most modern of maps at the turn of that century missed the southern tip of the lake by some ten miles, allowing Ohio to claim the land that would later become known as the Toledo Strip. By the time later generations of cartologists more accurately placed the lake on their maps, Ohio had already put down their fenceposts, occasionally literally; but more importantly, in the words of a state constitution that had been approved and vetted by Congress.

By the 1820s, both the Michigan Territory and the State of Ohio laid claim to some 468-acres of midwestern woodlands, a wedge of land that came to a point at Toledo. Both of them wanted the land. Needed it. Political posturing between the two jurisdictions was fierce. Both made to quickly set up governmental operations in the disputed area, and both passed laws making it illegal to do any kind of official business with the other. Handfuls of residents in the disputed territory were arrested by Michigan for identifying as Ohioans. Handfuls more were arrested by Ohio for identifying as Michiganders. It was an impossible existence, eased only by the fact that for several years, neither entity remembered to collect taxes in the Toledo Strip.

When Toledo was founded in 1833, it was founded as a Michigan town, but not without controversy or debate. The residents of the young village seemed to believe they would get to choose which state they'd belong to, and in the end, maybe they did.

But not before they changed their minds.

Among Toledo's founders was an entrepreneur and land speculator named Benjamin Franklin Stickney. Stickney had purchased expansive plots of land around the Maumee River, envisioning development of hydropower and canal projects that promised to make Toledo the kind of midwestern gem that would make him a ton of money.

With stars in his eyes, Stickney made early plans to keep as much of that profit as he possibly could. The Michigan Territory had more friendly tax rates than Ohio did, and so Stickney led the charge to build Toledo as a place in Michigan.

At the same time, Michigan was preparing the paperwork to apply for statehood, counting the residents of Toledo among its requisite 60,000 population, then petitioning the Congress for admittance to the Union.

Ohio would not have it. The Toledo Strip was theirs and had been for some time, as far as they were concerned. Possession was nine-tenths of the law, after all, and the remaining tenth belonged to the powerful. As an already established state, Ohio had all of the power too.

They lobbied and brokered deals to delay Michigan's statehood until the Toledo Strip had been ceded to them. For its part, Michigan was not in a ceding mood. Led by a hotheaded 22-year-old governor named Stevens T. Mason, the Michiganders made it known that there would be war before there would be surrender.

Ohio governor Robert Lucas called Mason's bluff.

Mason wasn't bluffing.

In the middle of it all was Benjamin Franklin Stickney, a man with a great name who had repented of his earliest opinions and found himself now solidly in the Ohio camp. It wasn't that he'd decided he was loyal to Ohio, just like he hadn't been loyal to Michigan in the first place. It was all about how much money he could make and keep then, and it was all about how much money he could make and keep now.

Stickney had heard the whispers that Michigan's leaders wanted to leave the Toledo area deliberately undeveloped, fearful that the growth of this new city would threaten Monroe, which wasn't far and was already well-established.

The decision threatened to bankrupt Stickney's holdings and so he pivoted in a moment, becoming among the loudest voices demanding that Ohio hold the Strip. Stickney Avenue cuts a line four miles through Toledo to honor one of the city's earliest heroes, but his betrayal quickly made him Michigan's Judas. Stickney was arrested by a Michigan militia, and when he refused to go peacefully, the armed men literally tied him to his horse and marched him back to his incarceration in Monroe.

Later on, when they tried to arrest him again, Stickney found himself right in the middle of the only bloodshed of the Toledo War. When Deputy Sheriff Joseph Wood arrived to apprehend Stickney, the whole family rushed to their patriarch's defense. Stickney's first son, One, got between his father and his captor. His second son, Two, stabbed the sheriff with a pen knife. Yes, those are their very real, legal names; and no, there is no account of how Stickney's daughter, Indiana, contributed to the struggle.

The Stickneys found themselves on the lam, more hopeful than ever that Ohio would win the Toledo Strip once and for all. The doctors had already proclaimed that Wood's injuries were going to prove fatal, and if Ohio didn't win the war, that would mean Two Stickney would be charged with murder in the state of Michigan.

As for Wood, he was bleeding out in a sickbed, and the doctor at his side could only prescribe a massive quantity of whiskey to take the edge off of the man's pain so that he could die in peace. Wood put away most of a jug of the stuff before he finally fell asleep and waited to expire.

The sheriff was probably more surprised than anyone when he woke up the next afternoon. He wasn't dead, but he might have wished he was. Somewhere in a cabin in frontier Toledo, Joseph Wood was nursing one of the most epic hangovers in American history. He would recover from the stab wound before he'd recover from the pharmaceutical alcoholic binge of the same night.

The incident might have seemed to be the prelude to a very real war, but it was more complicated than all of that. Ohio was understandably gun shy about marching into any sort of actual battle. Michigan was a United States territory and not yet a state. As such, any attack on Michigan would be considered an attack on the nation at large. For Michigan's part, it was still trying to gather support for its own bid for statehood. Demonstrating a willingness to attack and invade other states was not going to help its cause.

At a national level, policymakers seemed content to ignore the issue, but when they spoke out, they were most likely to speak out in favor of Ohio, a state that actually had the votes politicians were trying to curry, while Michigan was allotted an unvoting and unspeaking representative during Congressional proceedings.

The unspoken consensus was that Michigan had every legal right to the Toledo Strip, but that Ohio had every political recourse to take it. Former President John Quincy Adams described it best:

"Never in the course of my life have I known a controversy of which all the right so clearly on one side and all the power so overwhelmingly on the other."

Andrew Jackson, then the current President, postured as if he didn't have an opinion on the matter either, and Jackson was a man who *always* had an opinion. But for his part, he chose to leave the issue to the Congress and the courts, refusing to wade into the fraught political waters until whispers of war grew into full-blown choruses. It was only then that he acted, removing Stevens T. Mason from the Michigan territory's governorship. It was an unpopular move in Michigan, and the men up north would elect Mason as the state's first real governor as soon as they got the chance.

By then, Michigan had been pushed to a brink, tired of being threatened and bargained with by a political system that held all of the cards. It hurt to do it, but they didn't have any choice. They offered to make a deal. The final offer that came from the Feds wasn't the bargain they'd been hoping for, but it would have to do.

In exchange for ceding the Toledo Strip, Michigan would be allowed statehood, and as a consolation prize, they'd receive 9,000 square-miles of land north of the Straits of Mackinac. Michiganders viewed the whole thing as a raw deal at first, and there was even a faction of Michiganders who turned on Governor Mason, accusing him of cowardice, duplicity, and treason. As far as they were concerned, he'd conceded the unimaginable commercial wealth of the Toledo Strip for a frozen and barren wasteland on the other side of a lake that wouldn't see a bridge for another century.

The charges wouldn't stick to Mason, and it wouldn't be long before the deal became a coup for Michigan. It was just a few years after the end of the Toledo War that iron and copper were discovered in those northern lands, ores that delivered on a promise to make the state wealthy.

So, in the end, Ohio got Toledo and Michigan got the Upper Peninsula. On January 26, 1837, Michigan was officially admitted as the 26th state in the Union and Stevens T. Mason was back in the Governor's seat at the ripe age of 25.

It's all a very long-winded tale designed to explain why you're about to read about an 80-mile bike ride through Ohio in a book about Michigan.

*   *   *

The sun rises over the Huron and brings with it a daydream summer tailwind that will make riding today's course a breeze in the most literal way. But first, there are just a few urban miles into that wind in order to discover a bit of Michigan that would be easy to miss. There's a small bit of land out here that is still Michigan, the Lost Peninsula, a casualty of that east-west line drawn from the southern tip of Lake Michigan.

There are exactly 250 acres of land on the Lost Peninsula and about 140 people who live there. They are cut off from the rest of their state, and their land is accessible only by travelling through Ohio. It might have made logistical sense for Michigan to cede this land to Ohio, too, but in the aftermath of the Toledo War, they weren't about to give up another inch. For nearly two centuries now, they haven't.

The children of the Lost Peninsula climb every morning onto school buses that will jump a pair of state lines on the way to school and again on the way home. Newlyweds make the trip out of their state and back into it again to get a marriage license. There's a whole new problem around the issue of recreational marijuana, legal in both Ohio and Michigan, but illegal to transport across state lines.

It's an illicit confusion with roots all the way back to Prohibition, when rumrunners would sneak across the lake from Canada and into the Lost Peninsula to deposit their contraband. Outside of Ohio's jurisdiction and beyond the convenient patrol routes of Michigan's cops, the Lost Peninsula was a wet haven in a dry nation for most of the 1920s.

Now it's a place that's fully gated to their neighbors from the south, less a consequence of the still raging rivalry between Michigan and Ohio and more to deter a parade of tourists interested in driving through the quiet neighborhood to observe the geographic curiosity. We're left to watch the Lost Peninsula from the outside in, and it's the closest we'll get to Michigan for the rest of the day.

We pedal west through urban Toledo, a border city if there ever was one. They drink Vernor's here. Detroit pizza has found an outpost in Toledo, but Cincinnati chili has not. The Detroit Red Wings and the Detroit Tigers both have minor league affiliates in Toledo. And despite the fact that neither professional football squad has given their fans much to root for until very recently, I count a pretty equal number of Lions banners and Browns flags. It's an hour from Toledo to Detroit, two to Cleveland, two-and-a-half to Columbus, and three to Cincinnati.

The stop and go of Toledo's city limits gives way to the well-manicured bike paths of the suburbs, and we roll past an enormous youth soccer tournament where it costs $20 just to *park* in the designated lots. Entrepreneurial homeowners are charging even more for a spot in their driveways. It doesn't seem to matter if you're in Michigan or Ohio or anywhere else. The suburbs are the suburbs wherever you go.

But they don't last for long, and soon enough, the landscape is filled with Ohio farms that have forgotten their Michigan roots. We roll through tiny towns that are idyllic, quaint, and well-planned, exactly the way that Ohio would want them. The town of Metamora is home is home to a handful of well-gridded streets, fewer than 600 people, and a town flag that is literally an empty bench beneath an oak tree.

But this isn't a book about cute Ohio towns, and those aren't the kinds of things we rode our bikes all this way to see. Seven miles west of Metamora we stop at exactly the kind of intersection that doesn't seem to invite loiterers, and we pause at a historical marker to remember the only battle of the Toledo War.

At the height of the controversy between the states, the only real action came with expensive and repeated attempts to resurvey boundary lines based on coordinates marked down in different maps. Michigan launched a survey based on one map. Ohio launched one based on another. The Federal Government sent soldiers to do a second survey based on Ohio's specifications.

It was a waste of time and money. There were never questions or doubts about the quality of the surveyors who'd marked the boundaries. The only question was about the terms those boundaries were founded on. Sending out men to retrace the lines over and again was exactly the kind of thing that accomplished nothing and appeased nobody but allowed the government to claim to the people that they were acting decisively.

None other than Robert E. Lee got himself involved as a soldier-surveyor during the tenuous bits of the Toledo War; neither the most important nor most famous conflict between the states that he'd find himself involved in.

After the first two surveys solved nothing and changed nothing, Stevens T. Mason and the rest of the Michiganders had had enough. They claimed the Toledo Strip for their own and declared that anyone caught on their land doing any kind of surreptitious survey work on behalf of the Ohioans would be subject to arrest.

Governor Lucas knew the threat, but once again, he called their bluff, sending the survey crew anyway.

Once again, they weren't bluffing.

When the survey crew stopped to rest for the night on the land of Colonel Eli Phillips, they couldn't have known they were about to participate in a war. But then, they probably didn't know

46

that Phillips was a proud Michigander on disputed land. And they definitely didn't know that Colonel Eli Phillips was a part of the Michigan militia.

Imagine the fright of the surveyors when their assailants burst from the woods without warning, brandishing weapons and threats. Armed primarily with compasses and tripods, the survey crew fled the scene, bemoaning the lack of hazard pay in their contracts and abandoning their equipment as they ran.

The Michigan men fired shots in the direction of the runaways. None of the shots connected. It's not known if they were intended to. The Michigan militiamen ran down the meticulous measurement men, and the posse rounded up and arrested nine of the surveyors by the time it was all said and done. The whole episode would become known as the Battle of Phillips Corners, and besides Two Stickney's stabbing of Sheriff Joseph Wood, it was the only real action of the Toledo War. There was exactly one battle in the Toledo War, and Michigan won it.

But Ohio had a sophisticated spin machine working on its side. Mature newspapers wrote op-eds that trickled into markets across the nation, and the picture they painted of their Michigan neighbors was not a complimentary one. The story went that the Michiganders were untame and unpredictable, led by a foolhardy Boy Governor who was punching far above his weight.

The story that was told of the Toledo War was not one of Michigan victory, but one of unchecked and unwarranted aggression. After all, it was an armed militia attacking a group of geometry-minded surveyors, not exactly the scenario that called for a shoot-first-and-ask-questions-later strategy.

Michigan men came from wild lands and wore wild beards. They were an affront to the gentility of Ohio – and America. They didn't have a term for it yet, but if they had, they might have called Michigan the Wild West or the Wild North. As it was, Ohio journalists would need another term to describe the wild and feral nature of the Michiganian aggressors. They would need a newsworthy nickname that would paint them as unkempt woodsmen who lacked the manners and nuance of the Ohioans they stood so brazenly against. From then on, the Ohioans would refer to the men from the north as the Wolverines.

The moniker stuck, and the good people of Michigan would like me to be sure to mention that as we stood at Phillips Corners in June of 2024, the Michigan Wolverines Football Team were the defending National Champions, and maybe even more importantly, that they beat Ohio State to get there.

It's a rivalry so fierce that their annual contest doesn't even need a clever moniker or gimmicky trophy to raise its stakes. They just call it The Game, and the only dressing up it needs is a pair of capital letters. It's another battle that Michigan can claim as a victory, with a 62-51-6 record since 1897.[2] Online lists generally count the storied feud as one of the two or three fiercest rivalries in American sports, and that's often without knowing that The Game has roots in an early American civil war.

In a lot of ways, the Toledo Strip still feels like disputed territory. Michigan banners fly proudly and more frequently the further west we get. The Battle of Phillips Corners was fought 60 miles from Ann Arbor and 160 from Columbus. A garage outside Lyons is painted boldly in maize and blue, and by the time we get to Pioneer, we're passed by a black truck with a vanity plate that says WLVRNS and that proudly displays a championship flag riffling in the wind.

---

[2] This book was written in 2025, before the 2025 edition of The Game was played.

This is Ohio's land and maybe it always has been. That much has been settled for some time now. But there are still plenty of people in the Toledo Strip excited to shout an anthem for Michigan, and they've always been here too, hailing their victors valiant, cheering with might and main, and saluting their conquering heroes at any opportunity.

You can't be called the loser of a war if the war's still going, and every November, when hostilities are continued on the gridiron, it's a reminder that this war's not over yet and there are still more battles to be won.

CHAPTER FIVE
(MORE) DISPUTED BORDERS

We're awake at a hotel in Angola just in time to drink bitter coffee in our third state in as many days. This one is Indiana, another of the places that drew lines somewhere those lines were never supposed to be. At least it can be said that this border dispute was a little more civil than the one that sparked the Toledo War, even if it remains a little less resolved to this day.

The truth is that Indiana came for Michigan's land first, nearly twenty years before Two Stickney brandished his pen knife in that saloon. Unlike Ohio, Indiana did not try to claim the land with subterfuge, trickery, and force. It simply petitioned the Congress, and the Congress acceded.

Indiana's argument was straightforward enough. It had no direct access to the Great Lakes. The Michigan Territory had plenty. Indiana asked to take ten miles from their northern neighbor's southern boundaries to have for its own. In sum, it represented about 1,400 square miles, three times as much as what would later become the disputed Toledo Strip.

The Michiganders didn't put up too much of a fuss over this first seizure of their land. Maybe it's because there wasn't much within that stretch of land that seemed promising, certainly nothing as lucrative as what was imagined for Toledo. Maybe it's because they were not yet too jaded to play nice. Maybe they were persuaded by Indiana's argument that to landlock their new state would doom them to be just another Kentucky, a fate Michigan would not wish on anyone.

Or maybe it's because they couldn't put up a fuss. As a territory, Michigan delegates were permitted only to observe the goings-on of their nation's congress. They couldn't vote. They couldn't speak. When things didn't go their way, they could either throw up their hands or take up arms. When it came to the Indiana question, they threw up their hands.

They wouldn't do it again.

Either way, our bike ride begins in the parts of Indiana that weren't originally planned to be there, and as any proper northern Indiana cyclist will tell you, all of the best bike rides up here point directly into Michigan as quickly as possible.

That's exactly what we do, a few quiet northerly miles on flattened Hoosier roads before we cross a state line that comes with much less pomp than a similar crossing delivered between Ohio and Michigan the day before. That's not to say that there aren't differences between Indiana and Michigan, because there are, and there are plenty of them. Those differences are just less pronounced, and the roads that connect the two states pretty much just blend into one another. The vibe of northern Indiana exists in a nebulous margin between Ohio and Michigan, a description that does not sound like a compliment and is not meant as one.

At least it's not long before it's over and we're pedaling back through the state that this book was supposed to be about in the first place. Our team has been diminished by two. Andrew is back at his day job and Erin is back at hers. For the first time, Ashley and I are really on our own out here, no help, no friends, no car to call on in case of emergency. It's a sudden independence that couldn't have come at a worse time.

Among the many repercussions of the unchecked avarice of Michigan's original lumber barons came the extinction of species, the eradications of habitats, and the complete destruction of any kind of a forest that might shield a pair of cyclists from the massive block headwind that barrels down at us from the west. The howling wind comes in stiff and rigid gusts, blowing from the edge of Lake Michigan all the way to Lake Erie. I am sure the scent of Chicago dogs has carried all the way from Illinois. We hunch over our bikes, laboring against the very same air we're breathing and take turns hiding out behind each other's butts because there is nowhere else to go.

I'd promised Ashley a short and easy day today. It's not the first time I've lied about the nature of a bike ride, and it won't be the last. Believe me when I tell you that this was brutal.

*   *   *

For as much as the Ohioans tried to paint their northern neighbors as aggressive, temperamental, ruffian wolverines; the truth is that the men from Michigan aspired – at first – to be none of those things. As a territory, Michigan's earliest interactions with its nation were passive and accommodating. Happily giving up the northern ten miles of Indiana showed a willingness to cooperate and compromise; an appeasement that ought to have put the Michigan Territory firmly within in the good graces of the leaders of the United States.

When that didn't turn out to be enough, there was always outright pandering and brownnosing, a strategy that Michigan adopted long before the Toledo War. If the text of actual written laws wasn't enough to persuade President Jackson and his staff to lobby on Michigan's behalf, then maybe some calculated butt-kissing would do the job.

As soon as we cross back into Michigan proper, we find ourselves in Branch County, named after Jackson's Secretary of the

Navy, John Branch. This is one of ten counties in Michigan named after Jackson and his cronies, a strategy openly designed to gain their favor during the first salvos of the Toledo War.

John Branch never visited Michigan as far as we're aware, and he made most of his political fame as a North Carolina senator and Florida governor. Branch County, Michigan is the only place in the country that's named after him.

The rest of the Cabinet Counties tell different stories, but almost none of those stories run through Michigan. Berrien County is named after a prodigious slaveholder from Savannah. Livingston County is named after a Louisiana congressman.

As for the flattery, it obviously didn't work, but it wasn't for lack of trying. In fact, if it hadn't been for an early sex scandal that rocked Andrew Jackson's White House, maybe everything would have turned out differently.

The controversy began when an indebted sailor named John Timberlake died at sea aboard the USS Constitution, leaving behind a young widow named Peggy and a pair of young daughters. The controversy grew when Peggy remarried just nine months after Timberlake's death, this time to Andrew Jackson's Secretary of War, John Eaton (Eaton County). According to the social norms of the day, it was an all-too abbreviated mourning period, unbecoming of the young widow, and especially unbecoming of a supposedly dignified member of the Presidential cabinet.

It would appear that the bar for what constituted a sex scandal was much lower back in the day.

Still, it was enough for the whispers to begin. When the rumors spread that Eaton and his new wife had been something more than cordial in the months leading up to John Timberlake's death, those whispers spilled into the print of the society columns.

And when it was revealed that Eaton had pulled strings to get Timberlake assigned to a four-year term on the vessel where he would die, those columns moved onto the front pages. A David and Bathsheba story was played out in Jackson's Cabinet meetings, in gossipy papers, and especially in the Washington social circles that Cabinet wives were expected to participate in.

Floride Calhoun, wife of Vice President John Calhoun (Calhoun County) appointed herself chief of the D.C. morality police and made it her mission to ostracize the Eatons at every possible turn. Calhoun refused to speak to the Eatons, did not invite them to her parties, and recruited a clique of other Cabinet Wives to do the same. For Calhoun and her mob of mean girls, it was of the utmost importance that they prevent Peggy Eaton's acceptance into higher society at any cost.

It would turn out to be a bigger cost than they expected.

Bickering among the Cabinet Wives spilled into Cabinet affairs, leaving Jackson's administration in very literal shambles. Things became so heated that Cabinet meetings occasionally devolved into shouting matches and threats of violence. At one point, Eaton even challenged Secretary of the Treasury Samuel Ingham (Ingham County) to a duel. Ingham declined.

By 1831, things had gotten so bad that Jackson asked for – and received – the resignations of every single member of his Cabinet, except for Postmaster William Barry (Barry County). Calhoun resigned as Vice President and was replaced by Martin Van Buren (Van Buren County).

Besides the obvious turmoil in the Executive Branch, the Eaton Affair would ruin a number of promising political careers. Calhoun, who had once been considered the heir apparent to the Presidency, was never a serious candidate for that office again. John

Eaton had once been such a promising politician that he was somehow elected Senator before meeting the position's age requirement but would only receive a handful of Presidential appointments for the remainder of his career. He never won an election again at any level.

As for Michigan, their attempt to woo Washington's policymakers was probably doomed from the start, but it was absolutely doomed by the end. They'd named ten counties after members of Jackson's cabinet in order to secure their favor, and by the time they needed to cash in on that goodwill, almost all of those men were gone. The Toledo War began in earnest the year after the Eaton Affair ended.

It took decades of legislation, appeasement, politicking, flattery, war, and compromise to finally determine Michigan's actual boundaries. No state in the nation has dealt with as much drama just to determine exactly where its lines start and end.

That's what makes it so surprising when you learn that they still don't know exactly where the lines are.

The insanity of the Toledo War and its multiple surveys ended with pretty distinct state lines with Ohio, marked with extant granite posts. A hundred years later, a dispute with Wisconsin led to a survey in the Upper Peninsula and the erection of concrete markers that delineate clear lines. Most of the rest of the state's boundaries are marked by obvious shorelines.

But the Indiana line hasn't been surveyed or marked since 1827, measured with antiquated and primitive equipment, then dotted with wooden markers that have rotted away to nothing in the last two centuries. The Indiana state line is an approximation, not much more than a series of best cartographic guesses and a set of traditionally held home addresses.

As we continue to ride our bikes into the screaming headwind, we're probably in Michigan, but who knows? Maybe this is Indiana. Either way, the wind doesn't seem to care.

If it's a dispute, it's a quiet one, and there doesn't seem to be much political will to upset the status quo. There has been some discussion and some funding allocated to establish proper state lines, but probably not enough discussion or funding to do the job completely and correctly. The border between Indiana and Michigan is a long one filled with sand dunes, wetlands, farms, river crossings, and even the occasional feral forest. Into the headwind, I can't help but point out that those feral forests aren't occasional enough.

It's unlikely that too many properties and neighborhoods will move from one state to another when the survey is complete, but it's not impossible, and maybe this is the reason it's taken two centuries to get the effort off the ground. It's an awful lot of money to spend on a project that at best will change nothing, and at worst, could disrupt people's lives in profound and significant ways. A whole host of laws change when you cross that invisible line or when that invisible line crosses you. It's not just recreational marijuana and U-turns either. Everything from parental custody enforcement to car insurance regulations are a different animal in Indiana.

That having been said, if anyone ever hits oil within 1,000 feet of the commonly accepted state line, that land will be hotly disputed in a hurry. And if that ever happens, it means the disputed land will probably include my house.

By the end of this ride, I don't care if I live in Indiana or Michigan. I'm just glad to be home. My legs are empty, and my shoulders are screaming after hunching deep over my handlebars in an attempt to cheat the laws of aerodynamics. It's not impossible to consider that my shower is in one state and my bed is in another.

And if they are, then the short walk between those two places will be the best crossing of any state line I've made all week.

Ashley and I will sleep in our own bed tonight.

We won't see it again for a while.

CHAPTER SIX

WHEN WE GET TO CHRISTIANA CREEK

There's an unfortunate coda that sticks to the end of the tale of the Michigan Cabinet Counties and their celebrated namesakes. Almost immediately after those counties became established places, they also became some of the most important spots on the Underground Railroad. Some of the Cabinet Counties would be an escaped slave's penultimate stop on the way to Canada, the last American place they'd ever lay their heads before leaving the nation forever. Others of the Cabinet Counties would become final destinations, unimaginable enclaves of freedom and opportunity that were decades ahead of their time. The nomenclative tragedy of all of this is that the Cabinet Counties, in almost all cases, were named after unashamed and unapologetic slaveowners.

The Jackson White House's official position was to preserve the institution of slavery, and Jackson himself enslaved more than 40 human beings. Eaton, Berrien, Livingston, and Branch all kept slaves. John Calhoun, who is pictured on Wikipedia as the cursed offspring of a werewolf and a vampire, reinvented himself as a proslavery extremist after resigning the Vice Presidency. Calhoun was among a small number of loud voices seeking not just to preserve the institution of slavery, but to expand it.

Perhaps the saddest bit of all of this is that, unlike in many places, these unsavory fellows do not need to be remembered or recalled to tell the full account of Michigan's history because they were never a part of Michigan's history.

None of them really, except one.

Lewis Cass, pictured on Wikipedia as the kind of man whose skin is actively trying to run away from his face, stepped into John

Eaton's seat as Secretary of War in the aftermath of the Eaton Affair. When Michigan named a county after him, Cass County was added to the list of Cabinet Counties, but this occasion was different. This time, they weren't trying to woo Lewis Cass. They were legitimately trying to honor him.

Cass had been the territorial governor of Michigan for nearly 18 years by the time he received the call to join the Jackson administration in D.C. He'd seen Michigan through its most formative years, and in fact, he'd been the man behind the strategy to name all of those other counties after Jackson's cabinet members to begin with. The gambit might have won Cass more of the President's esteem than it won his state.

Either way, Cass made the move to Washington and George Bryan Porter, pictured on Wikipedia as an extra from *Grease*, took over the territorial governorship. Among his first moves was one to name a county after his predecessor, and that's where we're riding our bikes now.

These are home roads for us, the places we spin on weekdays, the coffee shops we visit on weekends. There's the Baker's Rhapsody in Dowagiac. There's the Savage Bean in Cassopolis. There's a Bigby with a drive-thru that we had to walk through more than once during the Covid pandemic. I've spent more of my life cycling through Cass County than anywhere else in the world, never needing a map, always knowing where the hills are when I want to find them, and more important, knowing where they are when I want to avoid them.

This is familiar turf and the thing about familiar turf is that it's easy to take it for granted. But Cass County is the kind of place that should never, ever be taken for granted. And when you're on its roads, you should always remember exactly who was here before you, because their stories are too important to ever be forgotten.

It's a story that begins in 1836 when a group of southern Quakers relocated to Cass County, citing their stringent abolitionist values. They had spoken openly about the evils of slavery, but realized that their participation in an economy built on the back of slave labor was to be complicit in its practice.[3]

So they left.

But for the Carolina Quakers, it wasn't quite so easy. Carolina law maintained that freed slaves could be captured and returned to slavery, and indeed, there became a cottage industry in the recapturing of human beings who'd been set free by their enslavers. Many of the Carolina Quakers took toward buying up those slaves and providing them as free a life as possible without exposing them to the potential horrors of a resale.

The only problem, then, was that to leave Carolina for moral reasons meant leaving their slaves behind to an unknown fate. So when they left, they offered to bring the slaves with them. The first to leave was a white Quaker preacher named Henry Way. He moved to Calvin Township in Cass County and brought with him a freed slave named Lawson. Other Quakers would follow, sneaking word into southern slave communities that they were moving to Michigan, and that there would be home and opportunity for African Americans who could find their way there.

The echoes of the Quaker fathers of Cass County ring out along roads with names like Penn and Dutch Settlement. When the hills on Dutch Settlement go on and on and on, I remind myself

---

[3] Significant parts of this chapter are lifted from my second book, Ride the Jack Rabbit: More of the People, Places, & Events that Make Michiana Fascinating.

that turning toward a different route is not an option. I'm here for the history and the history necessitates the climbing.

By 1850, Cass County was a final destination along the Underground Railroad for many escaped slaves and a forever home for many freed ones. The Quakers of Cass County had kept to their word, offering land, friendship, and opportunity to anyone who would choose to call Cass County their home. And when they needed to, the Quakers went one step further in their hospitality.

Despite their stringent commitment to pacifism, the Quakers offered their protection. It wasn't a hypocrisy, nor was it a betrayal of their values. They simply valued abolition even more than they valued non-violence.

In 1847, when 30 armed men arrived from Kentucky to take back their escaped slaves, more than 300 Cass County residents were there at O'Dell's Mill on Christiana Creek to take on the fight. Perry Sanford was one of the slaves they had come for, and he remembered the night this way:

"That was one of the most exciting anti-slavery events that ever happened in Michigan. They came down in a body and captured nearly all the slaves in that section. You see, the slave owners knew this Quaker settlement and they knew it was headquarters for escaped slaves. They brought tobacco wagons with them in which to carry back the fugitives."

The slave catchers spent a few days in prison on charges of trespassing and disturbing the peace, but that was just the beginning of the drawn out legal process. Fearful that the trial wouldn't go their way, many of the freed slaves who'd been targeted chose to move away, mostly toward Battle Creek and into Canada. The bounty hunters were released one-by-one under shady conditions, and then the litigation began. In the end, none of the slaves were extradited back to Kentucky, although some of the Michiganders did end up paying restitution in court. They all agreed that it was a small price to pay to guarantee the freedom of their fellow man, and as for the slave catchers, Sanford recalled:

"They went home an awfully disgusted and mad crowd. They didn't take their old tobacco wagons back with them. Every morning, a wheel would be missing from those wagons, until every one had disappeared. Those wheels are now resting peacefully in the bottom of Diamond Lake."

The incident made the national news, drawing the ire of southern slaveholders and the admiration of many African Americans looking for an opportunity they could call their own. After all, very rarely did freedom mean anything like equality, and sometimes even freedom led back to bondage all over again. By their actions, the Quakers of Cass County showed that they were committed to a racial equality far beyond its time and well beyond abolitionism. It had begun with a handful of disgusted white Quakers and a few freed slaves, but now it had become a nationally known antebellum black haven.

Southern slaves began to hum a new song to themselves when they dreamed of their freedom: *When We Get to Christiana Creek*. They came in droves, and when they finally arrived in Cass County, it must have seemed too good to be true. They were welcomed with open arms by white Quakers and supported by free blacks who could commiserate with their own similar journey.

That's not to say that life was easy. It wasn't. For people who'd lived their entire lives in the deep south, contending with a frigid Michigan winter was a challenge unto itself. And even with the help of their neighbors, clearing mature forest and terraforming it into suitable farmland was a backbreaking labor at best. It was hard work, but it was real freedom, and just as importantly, it was real opportunity.

To call all of this unique would be an understatement. Even after the Emancipation Proclamation and in the aftermath of the Civil War, there were few places where blacks stood on anything like equal footing with their white neighbors. Sharecropping ruled the south. Segregation-based power dynamics ruled everywhere else. But in Cass County, and especially in Calvin Township, African Americans were proving that all they'd ever needed was a chance.

Cornelius Lawson was a descendant of the first freed slave to call Cass County his new home. By 1898, he was elected the Supervisor of the Township of Calvin. A few years later, black man Abner Byrd would be elected Town Clerk, and Matthew Artis would win a position as Treasurer.

By 1904, the rural enclave of Calvin Township held more black families than white ones, and more often than not, the African Americans were the more prosperous of the bunch. Surprisingly, this disparity did not seem to sow much in the way of discord between the groups, and according to the existing history of the area, race relations were far more positive than not.

It was a unique situation that drew the attention of researchers and activists from around the nation. Even among some abolitionists, there were questions about whether the slaves, once freed, had the capacity to thrive in a free and modern society. It was the mission of Booker T. Washington to prove that they could. Cass County would become his case study for the nation.

Washington came to Cass County, then stepped almost immediately into a carriage alongside the county's judge, a local newspaperman, and a prosperous African American farmer. Over the course of ten hours along the same Cass County country roads that I have traversed hundreds of times on bicycle, Washington noted impressive farms and well-kept homes.

Of course, Booker T. Washington was not surprised to see African Americans thriving in Cass County. As an activist, he would have expected to find the same success anywhere that his kinsmen would have been given half-an-opportunity. But he also knew he was writing for a skeptical audience.

Washington iterates that the African Americans of Cass County were up to the standard of their white peers in terms of financial well-being, moral and ethical righteousness, law-abidement, and church attendance. What he found and described in Cass County was more than provable prosperity, it was an equal adherence to traditional American ideals. The black pioneers were not just succeeding in reaching their own goals; they were succeeding in reaching and propagating the sacred American dream right down to the picket fence.

But then, Washington wasn't done yet. It was one thing to prove that the African Americans of Cass County were personally successful and personally righteous and personally accountable. It was another to show their commitment to civic responsibility and to the well-being of all people. For his skeptical audience, it wasn't enough to demonstrate that African Americans could do well for themselves. The bar was even higher.

Washington was left with the impossible burden of proving that the freedom of African Americans would provide a greater level of well-being for the white people around them.

It was a difficult argument, but once again, Washington struck gold in Calvin Township; pointing out the tax burdens paid out by wealthy African American landowners, businessmen, and agriculturalists throughout the county.

Washington appears to have been most impressed with a man named Samuel Hawkes, an African-American landowner, moneylender, agriculturalist, and real estate trader. Hawkes was notable as the single largest taxpayer in Calvin Township, owned about five hundred acres of land, and was worth at least $50,000. Adjusting for more than a century of inflation, Hawkes was a self-made and first-generation millionaire.

There exists in modern Cass County an army of volunteers who are committed to keeping this story alive. Underground Railroad Days are an important hallmark of the community's summer, and they take care to remember the important stories. More importantly, they take extra care to remember the experience.

There were men and women and children who crossed wild swamps for this, who only moved under the cover of night. There were people who buried themselves beneath piles of wool and burlap on the floor of a carriage that jostled through another impossible Georgia summer, and they endured it because Cass County was a place that was worth the suffering. They hid beneath floorboards in friendly homes, and slept beneath beds, but never in them. It was a fraught journey of weeks and months that was dangerous enough *even if they didn't get caught.*

We only had to push a headwind.

CHAPTER SEVEN

FOUR FLAGS

There are plenty of roundabout ways to wind up in Niles, Michigan. Driving 200 miles to Detroit and then cycling back across three states is certainly one of them. But it's nothing compared to the journey of Father Claude Allouez, a devout Catholic Frenchman whose influence is still felt across southwestern Michigan more than four centuries after he was born. The priest's piety would have made him believe that his evangelistic efforts could affect permanent change in the region, and his faith would not let him down. He wouldn't be surprised that the echoes of his work continue to reverberate throughout Michigan, even today. In fact, that's exactly what a faithful man expects.

But he might be surprised at the number of casinos he's indirectly responsible for.

Allouez was born in 1622 at Saint-Didier-en-Velay in France, surrounded by flowering prairies, terraced vineyards, and pristine rivers and streams that had been sourced in the high Alps. On clear days, Allouez might have seen those majestic mountains from his home.

Allouez spent the first three decades of his life in the shadows of those Alps, receiving his education at a college on their lower slopes, then spending 16 years cutting his teeth as a Jesuit novice at dozens of villages scattered along their idyllic ridges. It might have been how he happily spent the rest of his life, at least until someone noticed his knack for learning languages or when they realized how useful such a talent might be. In 1658, Allouez was a year beyond his era's average life expectancy, but somehow, his journey was just beginning.

Father Allouez received orders that sent him away from the only home and country he'd ever known and to which he would never return. The long trip across the Atlantic would give him plenty of time to learn as many Native American languages as he could, and he was going to need a lot of them. Among other things, his mission was to Christianize a wild place on the other side of an ocean that was still 200 years away from being called Michigan.

The Catholic evangelist bounced around French North America, settling first in Quebec, then following rivers and native trails west across modern-day Canada before dropping into what would later become Wisconsin and Illinois. He wound up in modern-day Niles, Michigan by the 1680s. It would be his final assignment, and it did not happen by accident.

White people had been in Niles before they'd been in Detroit, and there was a time when, of the two, the Niles area was certainly more important. Generations of Native Americans already knew the region as the onramp and offramp to the St. Joseph River, then among the most important and heavily travelled rivers in a sophisticated aquatic highway that crisscrossed the continent.

French explorateurs arrived in 1675 and recognized the area for what it was, a transportation and commercial hub of the Native American world. It was the kind of place that could bring a man profit and glory, and most importantly, the stylish skins and furs of tens of thousands of dead North American forest animals.

But trading couldn't begin in earnest right away. This was an area populated by several tribes speaking several languages, and the French explorers spoke none of them. So that was the logistical problem, and then there was the economic one: Before they could begin making deals, they would need something to offer the natives in return.

If they wanted to export pelts, they needed something to import. More often than not, that something was Christianity, and if it seems a little uncouth to push religious interest to drive financial gain, then it's at least worth remembering that their second-most common import was pestilence and disease.

Either way, the French saw Niles as a marketplace that could deliver almost limitless wealth. All they needed to realize that dream was a multilingual Christian-maker to build friendly relationships with the people who were already there.

Father Allouez arrived in 1687 and began the work of establishing a mission alongside the entrepreneurial commercial work of a handful of French profit seekers. For the French, economic development and evangelism were not inherently separate pursuits. There was a symbiosis there. Allouez established peaceable relationships that led to favorable trading arrangements. At the same time, he kept an eye out that the traders weren't exploiting his new converts too much, worried how shady business dealings might upset his disciple-making efforts. In exchange for his work as a religious intermediary, the local traders would support his work and keep him fed. As far as the French were concerned, it was an arrangement that let everyone win.

And at least for a while, it seemed like it was exactly that kind of relationship indeed. The French commercialists established preferential trading relationships that would later solidify as military alliances during the French and Indian War. And as for Allouez, he baptized some 10,000 tribal people, planting Catholic roots that would continue to bud for centuries to come in Native American communities across the region.

It was a lot of work for Father Allouez, made even more impressive by the fact that he did all of it in just two years. Allouez was already 65 when he arrived, and he would die at 67 in 1689. He is buried in Niles, and his gravestone might be the oldest in the entire state.

Allouez did not live to see the 1691 establishment of Fort St. Joseph at Niles, the epicenter of French trading operations in the region. The base wasn't erected to keep a tenuous peace or to quell any kind of localized uprising. There were no such problems, so far as we can tell. But at the same time, it seemed foolish not to create some level of protection for a place that dealt in so much wealth.

Fort St. Joseph was not built to launch great military attacks, and as we're about to find out, it was not built to withstand great invasions either. It was simply built to provide a small measure of protection for fur traders and French priests during a mostly friendly time. When the work was finished, it was a new priest who was tasked with delivering the benediction as the French flag was raised to the top of the pole, the first banner in a parade of them that would fly above the place that would become Niles, Michigan.

Of course, it wasn't the emblematic French tricolore we're familiar with today. The first versions of that famous flag wouldn't arrive for another hundred years. In 1691, France was still very much a Kingdom, and the Kingdom of France had a flag all its own – a stark white design covered in 86 golden fleurs-de-lis, and with some iterations featuring a pair of mostly naked baby angels hoisting a bejeweled crown atop another trio of fleurs-de-lis. As far as flag designs go, it's one of the busier ones.

That flag flew over the fort for seven decades until the British won control of Michigan as a prize at the end of the Seven Years' War. The British lowered the French banner and hoisted the Union Jack in its place in 1761, but they wouldn't hold the fort for very long either. The Brits had only just begun reestablishing Fort

St. Joseph as a peacetime trading post before they were forced to abandon it altogether when the Revolutionary War pulled their focus away from the middle parts of continent.

The area had so far followed a historical pattern that typified early Michigan. French rule gave way to British rule, and next would come the Americans at the end of the Revolutionary War, but before that could happen, there was another challenger for the land, and this one was entirely unexpected.

Enter the Spanish.

With the Americans and the British focused entirely on one another at battlefields hundreds of miles east of Michigan, a small Spanish contingent marched north from St. Louis to take whatever they could find. They knew full well that the other military forces on the continent were distracted with each other. They never intended to fight. They only intended to take. The Spaniards wound up at Fort St. Joseph in 1781, looted whatever they could find, then lowered the Jack and raised their own flag in its place.

The Rojigualda of modern Spain was not adopted until 1981, and so the Spanish bandera that flew over Niles was a different flag, a white one with a blood red St. Andrew's Cross. The raiders didn't stay long, taking their booty and heading back for St. Louis almost as quickly as they arrived. By the time anyone realized that the Spanish had been there, they were gone, and the Revolutionary War had ended in victory for the Americans. During the next century, the fort was wholly abandoned, lost to history, and swallowed by the forest.

The historic fort was not rediscovered until 1998 and has been an archaeological recovery site since 2002.

Today, Niles calls itself the City of Four Flags, and its crest features historic approximations of the fleurs-de-lis, the Union Jack, the St. Andrew's cross, and an American Betsy Ross. When most people tell the story of the Four Flags, this is usually where it ends.

It's also exactly where the controversy begins.

There's an entire history that is forgotten by the Four Flags, and you already know whose history got left out. Native Americans were here for hundreds of years and dozens of generations before the Europeans ever showed up. They tamed the land, formed alliances, and fought battles all their own before they even knew what a Frenchman was. They were here before the flags flew, remained throughout every changing of the guard, and watched with disinterest as the old Fort St. Joseph was taken back by the trees.

The Four Flags celebrate only the transient, shifting populations of the region while neglecting to mention the only groups who never, ever left; not even when tribes all over the Midwest were forcibly removed. That's a story that deserves to be told too, and it's where the Catholic roots planted by Father Claude Allouez begin to bloom all over again.

In the shadow of the torturous and inhumane Indian Removal Acts that were signed into law throughout the 1800s, Chief Leopold Pokagon made a strategic decision to save his particular tribe of Potawatomi Indians. By converting the entire tribe to Catholicism, he was able to earn his people a stay from removal. When every other native group was marched away, the Pokagon Band was permitted to remain. Today they operate four casinos in the region, contribute millions of dollars annually to tribal and local causes, count 4,300 citizens among their population, and are federally recognized as an Indian Nation.

It's that last part that's especially troubling for the traditional Four Flags story. According to the website of the City of Niles, the Four Flags moniker comes from the fact that "four nations have

72

controlled the area at different points during its 300-year history."
It's a troublesome quote to say the least. There's the obvious
Eurocentric native erasure that assumes the area has had a history
of just 300 years, and then there's the claim about those four nations.
As a nation, the Spanish can't really claim to have "controlled"
anything here. But the federally recognized Indian Nations who had
history here before the Europeans arrived? They certainly did
exercise control over the land, and for longer than any of their
antecedents.

The Four Flags commemorate 250 years of American rule,
70 years of French domination, less than 20 years of British
occupation, and about 40 minutes of Spanish interloping. The Four
Flags forget that the extant Native American population was the
only reason any of those people came here in the first place.

The Four Flags forget the only military conqueror that Fort
St. Joseph ever faced, and it wasn't the French, the British, the
Spaniards, or the Americans. The French built the fort peacefully,
the British acquired it tacitly, the Spaniards looted it sneakily, and
the Americans received the land it was on without ever knowing it
was there. None of them can claim to have taken the fort by force.

But the Native Americans can.

During Pontiac's Rebellion, the second siege of his Native
American alliance came at the land of the Four Flags. On May 25,
1763, they took Fort St. Joseph, killing a 25-man garrison, seizing
their commander, and claiming the fort for their own. The only
hiccup in the story is that Pontiac's forces didn't have a flag. It's not
known how long Native Americans held the fort before they left it,
but it was certainly longer than the Spanish did.

As for the city of Niles, it didn't arrive on the scene until the
1820s, and it's named after a guy who wasn't born until 1777, just

six years before the Four Flags narrative finally came to an end. The city has adopted the history of Fort St. Joseph as its own, although there's plenty of history in Niles that happened after the Revolutionary War. Niles was an early stop on the Underground Railroad and would later become home to the Dodge brothers, Ring Lardner, and Montgomery Ward.

As far as the cycling goes, Niles is a pretty great place to ride a bike. There's a lovely little bike path, some excellent pizza, and my favorite coffee shop in south central Michigan. Niles is a little gem of a city, but not such a sparkling one that you would expect several sovereignties to be in conflict for the privilege of keeping it. In fact, the first time I told my son that four separate nations had at different times tried to exercise control over this land, he told me that didn't sound like something that was true, and of course, he was right.

There were five.

CHAPTER EIGHT

THE WEATHER IN SOUTHERN MICHIGAN CAN CHANGE IN A SECOND

The way that lake effect snow works is basically this: In the early parts of the winter, when the frigid air is colder than the warm Great Lake it blows over, the temperature differential between the two causes a chain reaction that ends when a snowplow takes out your mailbox.

There's more to it than that, but not a lot more, and it's a meteorological phenomenon that's unique to the Great Lakes and a few other places scattered across the world. The oceans are too big, too deep, and too vast to experience significant temperature fluctuations during the changing of the seasons. Most inland lakes aren't large enough to appreciably influence the weather.

But the Great Lakes are unique. Lake Michigan has a surface area of 22,000 miles, but its water temperature is incredibly variable, reaching 70 degrees Fahrenheit in the summer and dropping into the 30s during the winter. As recently as 2014, 90% of Lake Michigan was frozen over during the bitterest parts of a long winter.

When a frosty December wind blows over a sleepy Wisconsin, the air temperature might drop into the 20s or teens. But when that same air finally reaches a lake that's sitting at a relatively mild 43 degrees, you have all the ingredients you need for a lake effect snowstorm.

Cold air and warm water form cloudy compromises for a hundred miles as the weather passes southeasterly over the lake. On the other side, thin bands of nimbostratus vapors blow intermittently, ready to make landfall, ready to dump inches and feet of snow, wherever they want, seemingly at a whim. Someone downwind is going to get hammered. It's forecasting who those someones will be that's the tricky part.

As capricious Michigan winds blow the system across the Great Lake, clouds are stretched lengthwise. Snowy payloads are concentrated into narrow blizzard-bringing strips, often just a mile across, and sometimes even less than that.

The result of all of this is that meteorologists can predict with some degree of accuracy *when* a lake effect snow event will occur but guessing where those snows will fall is more of a crapshoot. It's not at all uncommon to go to sleep at night with the promise of a weatherman's winter Armageddon, only to wake up to green grass and cleared streets. The snow day you were expecting? It came, just to a town six miles north of here. They got a foot-and-a-half of snow. You barely got a dusting.

Of course, if a warm lake can wreak meteorological havoc on Michiganders during the early winter, then it would stand to reason that a cold lake could wreak the same havoc during the early summer. This is when everything happens in reverse, warm western air conspiring with chilly lake water, then appearing on the mainland as intermittent clouds to deliver sudden temperature changes and popup showers on an otherwise beautiful day.

It's the kind of system that even the weatherman would have trouble seeing coming. At least that's what I'm telling my friends as they whisper epithets among themselves, not-so-silently planning a mutiny along the suddenly wet roads.

There are four of us on the road today. Ashley's here because she told me once that she would ride anywhere with me, a statement that will be put to the test before this course is through. Andrew's here, but he wishes he wasn't. And then there's my friend Bill, a retired newspaper reporter who spent most of the spring riding his bicycle in the mountains of Tucson, Arizona, training in a hot and hilly desert for every possible condition except exactly the one we're going to find ourselves in the middle of today.

I promise it was 70 and sunny when we set off.

Our route continues to dance across the modern Indiana state line but remains well north of the original one. We are in the unincorporated parts of Niles, Michigan and then into the unincorporated parts of South Bend, Indiana. We thread a needle between Galien and New Carlisle.

In Indiana, we're riding through LaPorte County, French for "The Door". In Michigan, we're riding through Berrien County, Confederate for "racist asshole."

Berrien is one of the Cabinet Counties, and while many of the Cabinet Counties were named after pretty objectionable men, John Berrien was unique among them. He was the most prodigious slaveholder of the group, claiming 143 humans among his taxable property in 1850. He was the most vocal defender of the institution, even making arguments to retain a loopholed version of the transatlantic slave trade 20 years after the import of humans was finally declared illegal.[4]

After his time in President Jackson's Cabinet, Berrien would serve parts of two terms as a senator from Georgia, and if anything, his views would become more radical. He was an early supporter of

---

[4] Even this "concession" failed to stop the transatlantic slave trade. The Act Prohibiting the Importation of Slaves was a toothless bill that did not include any penalties for guilty parties, and even worse, made no accommodations for what to do with human beings who'd been trafficked illegally. In practice, the captured Africans were taken in as wards of the state, *then auctioned off as slaves*, with the state keeping the proceeds for its coffers. It was this brand of state-sponsored slave selling that Berrien argued so fervently in favor of, ensuring that the import of human beings remained possible for another two decades beyond the time it was declared illegal.

the briefly lived Southern Party, an organization that pushed for secession years before it became fashionable to do so. When the Southern Party folded, he became a proud Know Nothing, espousing fear masked as a hatred for Jews, Catholics, Irishmen, and Germans.

So, no, I'm not a big fan of John Berrien, and at this moment, on this bike ride, I'm not such a big fan of Berrien County either, because now it's raining, a downpour that's arrived a full two hours before it was supposed to. Worse, it's brought with it a chill that I thought we were done with three months ago.

Potholes have become puddles, and bike tires throw wet grit that gnash between clenched teeth, then spit from wet mouths before any of it has a chance to become a pearl. It has all happened in the matter of a moment and all we can do is keep pedaling to the beat of the drubbing of the rain and the sharp snapperings of the chattering of teeth. Involuntary shivers race through exposed arms and legs, each new wave of chill shaking once-steady handlebars.

We're still 17 miles from New Buffalo, a tourist town if there ever was one on a day that has suddenly become frozen and rainy. At least there won't be a wait at the restaurant when we get there.

Many of the towns we'll see during the next week became tourist spots and vacation destinations after spending a century as an industrial hub or quaint farming community. But not New Buffalo. New Buffalo has tourism in its DNA, and it has since the very beginning.

In the late 1830s, the Michigan Central Railroad became the circulatory system of the Wolverine State, a grid of veins and capillaries that connected Mackinaw City, Bay City, Detroit, Windsor, Jackson, Lansing, Grand Rapids, and Kalamazoo as far east as Buffalo, New York. As for the other end of the tracks, those

78

ended in New Buffalo, not a destination unto itself, but instead the place where travelers from the east and the north could step off the train and onto a steamship that would take them the rest of the way to Chicago. Of course, the transition wasn't quite that easy, and the schedules of boats and trains rarely lined up so neatly. The connection might have taken a few hours or a few days depending on the conditions. Suddenly, every person travelling between Michigan and Chicago needed a bed in New Buffalo.

New Buffalo met the challenge, building hotels and restaurants and amusements along the lakeshore. They invited the tourists to stay and to put their feet up for a day or two. They made their town a comfortable layover and an easy place to spend money. New Buffalo was in the midst of a heyday, but it would prove to be a short one.

Eventually the railroad was run all the way to Chicago. New Buffalo was all but dried up from the moment the new line was opened. But some years later, it would come back, all because of the ease of travel *from* Chicago.

At first, there were only the trains and the boats. Then, in the early 1900s, there was US Highway 12. When wealthy Chicago industrialists would leave the noisy, dirty city in search of a place that was quiet, quaint, and beautiful; they'd end up in New Buffalo all over again.

It's hard to describe just how stark the difference is between New Buffalo and everything to the west of it. A drive out of Chicago on a Friday afternoon is a rush hour nightmare that lasts all the way through Gary and Michigan City, cars and congestion and the kinds of smoke-belching factories that still offer the signature pollutive haphazardness of the industrial revolution.

And then, just like that, you're in New Buffalo. The air is clean. The lake sparkles like a sapphire. There is no smoggy haze. There are no soaring skyscrapers. There are no dirty factories.

The sky is blue. The sun is shining.

Not on this day, of course. Not for those of us on our bikes. We haven't seen a blue sky or a sun ray in about an hour. It's been white-knuckle for a while now, an onomatopoeia of numb toes going squish-squish in wet shoes. It's the least excited I've ever been to see Lake Michigan. We emerge from around a set of tall Douglas firs only to get slapped in the face with an unobscured frozen lake wind and angry pellets of rain that are aspiring to become sleet.

We're delayed by a stoplight that only *feels* like it's never going to turn green, and then it's a short roll down Whittaker Street, New Buffalo's surprisingly democratic main drag. For a city largely built by and for Chicago money, New Buffalo doesn't boast of it. It's not a showy town nor an ostentatious one. There are luxurious homes back there, but they're *way* back there, good taste enough to stay off the beaten path.

New Buffalo's signature places are the kinds of egalitarian joints that don't have to dress themselves in too many trappings. There's Redamak's, a family-owned, cash-only burger joint that's favored by locals, travelers, and Jay Leno. There's Oink's Dutch Treat, a spartan ice cream counter where everyone waits in the same line, except maybe Joe Biden (he ordered chocolate chip) or Marisa Tomei (she ordered mint).

But we're not headed to Redamak's, and there's not anyone on this ride who wants ice cream. Instead, we're bound for New Buffalo's third landmark, The Stray Dog, and it cannot get here soon enough. The Stray Dog is a bar and grill, and if you're from the region, you've probably been there and you own the sweatshirt too.

80

As we roll to a stop in front of the place, there's a sense of relief. No one has died. There wasn't a mutiny. Erin is there with towels and dry clothes. We've made it, against the will of the whims of Michigan's capricious weather.

There's just one problem.

My hands don't work.

Here's the situation: I'm standing in a public bathroom, looking upon a neatly folded stack of my favorite warm clothes while I am literally trapped in a tightly-fitting, frigid, wet cycling kit. I do not know which circle of Dante's hell this is, but I have to imagine it's one of the narrower ones. My frozen fingers will not unzip my frozen bike jersey. In the bathrooms next to mine, my companions are trapped in the same circle. There may be a mutiny after all.

It feels like minutes of running my hands under the running water, not sure the temperature of the stuff, not sure if I'm burning my digits or freezing them further. But it must have worked. At last, I grip the zipper and fully enjoy the luxury of a fluffy towel. I have never been so happy to be naked in a restaurant.

Moments later, we're into our seats and ordering cups of chili before we even order drinks, more to hold the tiny bowls than to eat from them. I've never been alone in this restaurant before, and I've never seen the town so empty. Especially not on a Friday.

Even the weatherman didn't know this was going to happen, but it sure seems like everyone else did.

CHAPTER NINE
THE UNION PIER NUDIST CLUB

I'm not the first writer to wander off toward Lake Michigan with the unoriginally romantic idea that there's a great book just waiting to be discovered in the freshwater surf. Generations of authors and artists have made the trip to the Midwest's infinite blue – looking for an escape, a reset, or a shot of clarity in a world that's just too damn loud. They came to the lake to find sanctuary in the quiet woods, hoping that they could find transformation in the waters, dreaming that they could be someone different when they went back home again.

The incredible thing is that, sometimes, it worked.

It's hot as we ride north from New Buffalo, because of course it is. The weather has done the unthinkable, heating some thirty degrees overnight, cooking the still-wet roads, and turning the world around us into a sauna of a racecourse. Hundreds or maybe thousands of people who were nowhere to be seen the night before have flooded onto the streets, pointing themselves toward the beach or the boats or the bar. All of a sudden, New Buffalo is crowded, and sweaty, and loud.

A hundred years ago, the *proper* Chicagoans would have remained safely within New Buffalo's limits during their summer holiday. Even when the beaches and the restaurants were filled, as they will be today, it would have been out of the question to spill into the untamed villages just up the road, places that couldn't entertain a tourist and that, frankly, didn't want to. Anyway, those were the places the *improper* Chicagoans visited, the places that spawned rumors of naked orgies in lake-kissed forests, fueled by alcohol, early drugs, and Nihilist existentialism.

Today, there is no such delineation, and there is no such restraint. Modern tourism is a hungry, expansionist venture, one apparently led by an army of golf carts playing REO Speedwagon on the way to annex another tract of land in the form of a short-term vacation rental. It's a march that threatens the historic character of Michigan's small towns, many of which have become tourist destinations without ever intending to do so.

But then, that's not exactly a new problem.

Union Pier is less than four miles from New Buffalo, and the bike ride watches over the kinds of gorgeous lake houses that themselves have names. It's tough to say where New Buffalo ends and where Union Pier begins, and it's a mostly uninterrupted (and private!) residential road that sits between them. But in the years around the first World War, besides the thick forest that separated the two places, they might have been an entire world apart.

If New Buffalo was the neatly scheduled playground of Chicago's mainstream business class, then Union Pier became the summer escape of the city's counterculture, one built on the very same waters and for all of the same reasons.

They came to the lake because their work required at least as much quiet introspection as it did the frenetic chaos of the machine of the city. They came to escape the judgmental gaze of the urban elite, to love who they wanted to love, to live how they imagined they would want to live. They came to ingest whatever the hell they wanted, to wear whatever they wanted to wear, and more often than not, to wear nothing at all.

The more eclectic version of Chicago's summer migration might have started with the Jackson Park Art Colony. The self-appointed bohemians discovered Union Pier in 1913, at that point a small community filled with hardworking Lithuanians who lived on quiet beaches but had very little time to enjoy them. Maybe that last part was okay. The bohemians from Illinois would have enough enjoyment for everyone.

They flocked by the dozen to the still-wild sand dunes, swimming naked in the lake, men and women alike, discussing Nietzsche amid the flickering of a hundred nighttime fires. Before finding Union Pier, the Jackson Park bohemians had been the kinds of hypothetical artists more likely to debate than create, content to sit in brothel parlors and complain about the zeitgeist without bothering to put forth any alternatives.

But something happened to them when they came forth from the waters, born again of a bare-bottomed bohemian baptism just off the Union Pier beachfront. If they came for inspiration, they found it. If they came for renewal, they found that too. Once they wiped the sand from their feet and put on a proper pair of pants, they began to produce.

Sherwood Anderson came up from the waters, married a sculptor he met on the lake, and launched a writing career that saw him publish more than 40 books. Maxwell Bodenheim wrote his first verses for Chicago's *Poetry* magazine. Floyd Dell began writing plays. Margaret Anderson started *The Little Review*. After spending the better part of six years living like a medieval troubadour and trading his poetry for food on long walks across the county, it took a (skinny) dip in the lake before Vachel Lindsay finally settled down and started publishing.

But it was Ben Hecht who outdid them all.

For Hecht, the Nudist Club was practically a hermitage compared to the Chicago he would later recall, a place where he haunted "streets, whorehouses, police stations, courtrooms, theater stages, jails, saloons, slums, madhouses, fires, murders, riots, banquet halls, and bookshops."

He must have found the clarity he was looking for in the chilly waters of Lake Michigan, because after his time in Union Pier, Hecht set himself to the work of pen and typewriter, authoring some 45 books, multiple Broadway hits, and writing some of the most important screenplays in early cinema.

Ben Hecht won Academy Awards for his work on *Underworld* and *The Scoundrel* and enjoyed four more nominations between 1927 and 1948. He also worked on the original 1932 *Scarface* and the original 1937 *A Star Is Born*. He wrote a pair of Hemingway adaptations, *A Farewell to Arms* and *The Sun Also Rises*. He wrote two films for Alfred Hitchcock – *Spellbound* and *Notorious*. He worked with Frank Capra, Carole Lombard, Al Jolson, Marlon Brando, Cary Grant, and Howard Hughes. His final script was meant to be the first James Bond film, *Casino Royale*.

He collaborated with Louis Armstrong, was the ghostwriter for Marilyn Monroe's autobiography, and wrote a celebrated autobiography of himself. Hecht was played by Beau Bridges in a movie based on his life, and what a life it was. Born in New York, discovered in Chicago, and reincarnated in the waters of Lake Michigan; Hecht would go on to earn enshrinement in the American Theater Hall of Fame and the Chicago Literary Hall of Fame.

In 1939, filming was stalled on the set of *Gone with the Wind*, a work in need of serious revision before it would become the American classic that we know today. The holdup was costly for the studio, running up a tab of $50,000 a day while teams of writers tried to save a film that was drowning. Still stuck after several days and not sure how to rescue the script from itself, the studio sent for Ben Hecht, then known colloquially as The Shakespeare of Hollywood.

Hecht arrived on set and objected that he couldn't possibly rewrite the film as he hadn't yet read the novel. The studio told him there was no time to read the novel and stuffed the man in front of a typewriter. Hecht began rewriting the dialogues in one broken scene after another, surviving for a week on nothing but bananas, salted peanuts, and coffee. Working in 18-hour shifts, he completed the final script in seven days. Studio execs agreed that Hecht had saved the movie from box office disaster but failed to laud him with a writing credit on the film.

For all of the wonderful words that Hecht wrote during his long career, there is one more memorable than the rest. It was Hecht's decision to take the most famous line in *Gone with the Wind* and append a single word to the front of it: *Frankly*.

But neither that word nor any of the other pieces of Hecht's legendary folio were written until after the first time he stepped forth from the waters of Lake Michigan. Hecht and the rest of the Nudist Club would become the primary figures of Chicago's Literary Renaissance, none of them having published a word until after that first summer at the dunes. Chicago's historians will tell you that their Renaissance was a movement born in Jackson Park, and maybe that's true, but it's a movement that was reborn in Union Pier, Michigan – a parade of artists and writers and publishers each emerging from the waters and reentering the world the same way they came into it:

Completely naked.

It's almost enough to convince an aspiring writer that the only barrier standing between himself and massive success is the wearing of pants, but as we stand looking upon the magical lake from the Union Pier beachfront, Ashley tells me that we need to keep going and that it would be best for everyone involved if I would please put my clothes back on.

The Union Pier Nudist Club didn't persist for very long, and of course, a thing isn't beautiful just because it lasts. There were two wonderful summers on Lake Michigan in 1913 and 1914, but then that was it.

For those two years, the locals had been tolerant enough of the strange and naked bohemians, so long as the weirdos exercised the restraint to keep to themselves. Unfortunately, restraint had never been a hallmark trait of those revelers on the lake.

They finally flew too close to the shining Michigan sun when a handful of beautiful, nude bohemian women invited a handful of local men to join them for a dip and a tryst. It only took a few good Catholic husbands being seduced away from their families before the Lithuanians of Union Pier were forced to put a stop to the party. From then on, the Chicago bohemians would have to find a new spot to ply their eccentric and alternative moralities. For not the last time, Woodstock was over. It was time to leave, and so it was time for us to leave too, pedaling north on a bibliophilic journey that had only just gotten started.

It's been fewer than seven miles of cycling by the time we reach the town of Lakeside, but already we've already experienced a dozen stunning views of Lake Michigan and seen at least as many adorable free little libraries scattered in front yards and on street corners. Whether or not they're aware of it, each one belies the long literary legacy of its region. Maybe it's because the lake inspires the otherwise ordinary to put pen to paper or maybe there is something more primal in the dunes that bids the authors to come to them. Whatever it is, there is something undeniably bookish about this particular slice of southwestern Michigan, and that's before you inadvertently stumble onto William Shakespeare's childhood home.

Listen, I don't know what it's doing there either.

The 1924 Chicago International Livestock Exposition made plans for that year's annual meat show to be the grandest such exhibition of farm-raised animal carcasses. The organizers spared no expense, securing several high-profile visitors like President Calvin Coolidge and inviting marquee entertainers from across the nation. For reasons that I do not fully understand, they even commissioned a spot-on replica of William Shakespeare's childhood home to serve as The Meat Shoppe at the epicenter of the festivities.

The Meat Shoppe was only ever intended as a temporary structure, but the building was too much of a treasure to simply be destroyed and disposed of. When the Exposition ended, the building was carefully dismantled, shipped to Lakeside, then painstakingly reassembled on the grounds of the Chikaming Country Club. A century later, it's still there, and it's in pretty spectacular condition for a hundred-year-old structure that was only ever built to last a few months.

As for the Country Club, besides the Shakespeare House, it's got an impressive literary history of its own. Among its charter members were Jane Addams, founder of Chicago's Hull House and author of a dozen books of her own. In 1931, she won the Nobel Peace Prize.

Addams didn't swim with the Union Pier Nudist Club, but she would have certainly known about them. Lakeside is barely two miles north of Union Pier. All Chicagoans, Addams and the nudists would have taken the same trains out of the city, gotten off at the same station, and then marched in barely opposite directions to get to their final destinations.

That the western edge of Berrien County became such a marketplace of underground artists, philosophers, free thinkers, nontraditional governmentalists, and brokers of subversive ideas isn't something that happened on purpose, but it wasn't something that happened on accident either. This slice of the country was where Chicago's counterculture could speak openly about the things they'd only discussed in whispers back at home. Ideas that were fomented in the Windy City were fermented in southwestern Michigan, long before Berrien County became a celebrated wine region of its own.

That's why the Communists came here, hosting national conventions in 1920 and 1922 at nearby Bridgman, a few years after founding the party in Chicago. The first of those gatherings went off without a hitch. The second one was raided by the Feds.

The 1922 Bridgman Convention marked the end of an era for the consequential voices who'd so often frequented the region. The operation recovered scores of Communist documents and ended with high-profile arrests that made national headlines. Once southwestern Michigan became known as a secret hotbed of nontraditional ideas, it stopped being one, but not before it helped to produce some of the most consequential American writers of the first half of the twentieth century.

*   *   *

Harbert is a town from a different time, but then maybe it's not really a town. It's all dirt roads and old trees, mossy-shingled homes, a barn that used to be a dance hall and old-timers who remember when it was. The canopy is thick, the shade is ever-present, and the lake is close. Harbert is where Carl Sandburg used to live, and it's where he started some of his most important works.

The house is still there. I haven't been in it, but I've been in a house on the other side of the shady sand swept lane. I was drinking a Modelo as my host pointed out the important spots on a historic tour through his picture window. Over there were the goat farms. Next to that, the Prohibition era speakeasy.

"And over there," he gestured, pointing toward the modest second-floor balcony across the way. "That's where Carl Sandburg wrote *Lincoln*. Old-timers used to complain about him all the time."

"They complained?" I asked.

"Yep, he'd be out there for hours at a time all day all summer, and whenever he was writing…"

There was a tiny pause there, and I should have known what was coming next before he said it, but he said it anyway:

"He was completely nude."

CHAPTER TEN
THE LONGEST BRIDGE IN THE WORLD

You might know the town of St. Joseph, Michigan – if you know it at all – as the home of Silver Beach Pizza. That's where people go to wait for hours to eat some pretty excellent pizza inside an old train station while drinking beer from a frosty schooner that looks like the frozen version of Harry Potter's Goblet of Fire.

You might know it as the place the St. Joseph River spills into Lake Michigan, discovered by white men in 1669 and claimed for France when Robert de La Salle built Fort Miami at the place where the waters meet.

You might know it as the home of the Whirlpool Company, founded in 1911 by Louis Upton, a man you should thank the next time you don't have to use an old-timey washboard to get your shirts clean. You might also know it as the home of Upton's nephew, Fred Upton, a 14-time congressman from Michigan. Or maybe you know it as the home of Fred's niece, Kate, a four-time Sports Illustrated Swimsuit Issue cover model, which is how I was able to explain the content of my Google search history as research.

It's not a bad haul of famous names and places, but if things had been just a little different, the town might have been made famous for so much more. That's because, if not for a technicality, you might have learned about St. Joseph, Michigan as the site of the first motorized heavier-than-air flight.

Five years before the Wright Brothers put Kitty Hawk on the map, Augustus Moore Herring was at St. Joseph trying to beat them to the punch. The Michigan sand dunes made an ideal proving ground for Herring's adventures in hypothetical flights. He could launch himself from the high places, and in cases of catastrophe, which came more often than not, he could land in the soft sand or even softer lake water. For early aviators, powered flight wasn't just an engineering problem. There was also the matter of surviving one failed experiment in order to test another.

Herring survived many such experiments until he finally had a machine that could get airborne. He excitedly invited aviation pioneer Octave Chanute to St. Joseph to watch him make the flight. The pair met on October 10, 1898, at the Silver Beach Amusement Park. For some reason, Herring could not get off the ground, and Chanute would not give him a second chance, taking the train back to Chicago that afternoon.

Herring made a pair of successful flights in the ensuing days, one for seven seconds and another for ten seconds. That was 17 more seconds than anyone else would see for a while, but without a high-profile witness, Herring's achievement was pretty well buried. Even among those who believed his claims, there was still that technicality. The holy grail of aviation had been defined as an engine powered, heavier than air, human controlled flight. Since Herring's device didn't have a proper steering mechanism, the consensus was that his accomplishment had missed that last requirement.

Even if it was real, it didn't count.

Herring's name would be largely forgotten except in niche historic aviation communities. As for St. Joseph, it wasn't going to be known for the world's first flight. It would have to settle for washing machines and supermodels, and I suppose neither of those is a terrible consolation prize.

The bike ride from St. Joseph to Benton Harbor should be a relatively short trip, but it's made longer by the opening of a drawbridge, a problem that inlanders rarely have to consider. For my part, I still think watching a drawbridge open is one of the neatest things in the world, but then, I don't live here. For the people who do, I suppose it's just traffic, and it carries with it all the magic of getting stuck by a train or stopped by a funeral procession.

Soon enough, the boats are through, but just when we expect to start rolling again, we don't. After a moment or two, it's time to wonder if the person in charge of closing the bridge forgot to push the button. A car honks on one side of the broken road and then two more on ours. It's almost a literary shame when the bridge kicks back into action and the avenue becomes whole again, because it's hard to imagine a better metaphor for the relationship between St. Joseph and Benton Harbor than a bridge between them that someone wants to keep broken.

The jurisdictions are a part of a regional conurbation that the locals call the "Little Twin Cities", but it's worth noting that if these cities are twins, they certainly aren't identical ones. In many ways, Benton Harbor is an undeveloped negative of the city we just left. St. Joseph's population includes 84 white people for every hundred. Benton Harbor's includes 12. St. Joseph is a thriving tourist town boosted by the spending of tens of thousands of annual vacationers from across the Midwest. Benton Harbor recently spent six years under debilitating austerity measures set down by a state-appointed Emergency Financial Manager. Families in St. Joseph have a median income above $50,000. In Benton Harbor, it's less than half of that.

If St. Joseph is Kate Upton, then Benton Harbor is a man with ski goggles and no pants vigorously yanking at his pull start motorbike while absolutely housing a warm 2-liter of RC Cola.

Remember, Jacob and Esau were twins too.

It's hard to figure out how any of this can possibly happen, how everything can change from one side of a 300-foot bridge to the other, or how that same bridge can be colloquially known as the "longest bridge in the world" because either end feels like it comes from a different planet. But if you're looking for someone or something to blame, there's plenty of culpability to go around.

You could blame geography. There's St. Joseph, situated on its Edenesque bluff, a midwestern version of those shining European cities perched atop watercolor sandstone cliffs; and then there's Benton Harbor, down in the swampy lowlands at the bottom of the hill. There's a lot of blue on the flood plain map of Benton Harbor. There's a lot less on St. Joseph's.

You could blame the economy. St. Joseph is built on tourism, a financial engine that's proven to be as permanent and long lasting as the lake that drives it. Benton Harbor is – or was – built on the same kinds of manufacturing jobs that have been disappearing across Michigan for decades.

You could start with cartography. St. Joseph has more than four miles of shoreline. Benton Harbor has half of one.

You could start with politics. Benton Harbor's local politicians mismanaged its budgets and finances for years, and depending on who you talk to, the Emergency Financial Manager only continued the tradition.

Wherever you choose to start, all roads lead eventually to segregation and redlining, official and unofficial, on the books and off of them. Racism *probably* isn't the thing that sent Benton Harbor into its free fall, but it's definitely the thing that's kept it from getting back up again. There's not much left in Benton Harbor worth holding onto, but remarkably, in some places, there's still hope. Besides that, there's also an incredible history.

Believe it or not, Benton Harbor and St. Joseph were once bona fide rivals as tourism towns, siblings on equal footing. In fact, for a long time, before St. Joseph stole away the birthright, it was Benton Harbor who was the bigger, stronger brother.

Like the twins that they are, St. Joseph and Benton Harbor were founded at pretty much the same time, then incorporated as cities together in 1891. They fought bitterly over which of them should be chosen as Berrien County's seat, then quelled their burning tempers when it looked like neither of them might win the honor. Benton Harbor cast its votes in support of St. Joseph, bringing courthouse and commerce into its region, if not its city limits. St. Joseph has remained the county seat since 1894.

The sibling rivalry resumed immediately thereafter as each town set to establish itself as a premiere tourist destination. St. Joseph struck the first blow in the battle, opening Silver Beach Amusement Park in 1891 and adding its first roller coaster in 1904. Benton Harbor's counterpunch would come a few years later, and it would come from a most unexpected place.

*   *   *

Benjamin and Mary Purnell made quite a splash when they arrived in Benton Harbor, but then so does anyone who comes to a new place with a small band of loyal followers and immediately begins quoting the Book of Revelation. The Purnells claimed to be the seventh and final messengers of the church age, the ones who were chosen to sound their metaphorical trumpets to bring about the "accomplished mystery of God".

It was 1904 when the Purnells arrived in Benton Harbor with exactly seven followers, but within three years, their group numbered 700. The Purnells organized their followers into a commune they called The House of David and instituted a number of strict rules to govern the people who lived on their thousand-acre grounds. There was no meat, no alcohol, no tobacco, no haircuts, no shaving, no personal property, and absolutely no sex.

With all that out of the way, there was plenty of time for the members of the commune to get to work, opening a cannery, a laundry, a carpentry, a tailor shop, a zoo, and an electric works. Then, because maybe the trumpets weren't a metaphor after all, they started three brass bands and sent them on tours across the nation that could last for years at a time.

But as far as Benton Harbor was concerned, maybe the most important thing those hardworking, bearded, celibate vegetarians ever did was building the Eden Springs Amusement Park. It's the thing that put the city on the regional tourism map, and in no time at all, it was Benton Harbor – not St. Joseph – that became the premier destination in the region.

Eden Springs featured train rides, a zoo, and a bandshell. It invited families to stay in its rental cabins or on its campground. Eden Springs became the Disney World to Silver Beach's Universal Studios. You came and you spent a week at Benton Harbor's amusement park. You snuck down to St. Joseph's for a day if you had time.

For all of the restrictions placed upon them, life at the House of David might have seemed a pretty boring time, but that couldn't have been further from the truth. The commune members invested continually in their amusement park, adding new rides and new stage shows. They added a baseball stadium to their grounds, and more importantly, they added a baseball team to their ranks.

The House of David baseball team became the stuff of legend, crisscrossing the nation on grueling barnstorming tours, playing competitive games against amateur and semipro teams,

Negro League clubs, and even indulging in the occasional tilt with real major leaguers. Once they were established on the national stage, they even recruited a handful of future Hall of Famers to play with the club. Grover Cleveland Alexander and Mordecai 'Three Finger' Brown each played games on the House of David team, sporting real or fictional beards when they were on the field.

As far as 1920s tourist attractions go, it's hard to imagine much that could be better than watching Satchel Paige, at the peak of his powers, wearing a false beard while striking out a dozen minor leaguers at a matchup in Benton Harbor, Michigan.

There was probably a time when the people of Benton Harbor believed that the tourist dollars would never go away, that the strange religious folk would continue to bring travelers into the city for years and decades to come. But there was one problem with that assumption, and it was a significant one.

St. Joseph's tourism had been tied to its beaches, a guarantee so long as the fifth largest lake in the world didn't suddenly dry up. Benton Harbor's was tethered to the long-term tenability of a strange, personality-driven religious cult. One of those things was a better bet than the other.

You probably won't be surprised to learn that more than 13 young women came forward to testify that they'd been pressured into having sex with Benjamin Purnell while they were still minors. You probably won't be surprised that the story drew national attention and filled headlines in newspapers on both coasts. You probably won't be surprised to learn that the scandal shattered the community, driving a schism in its ranks, and watching over an exodus of its members.

You probably would be surprised to learn that Eden Springs remained open for another 45 years.

But as the commune dwindled, so did the quality of the park. They were slow to make repairs and slower to make improvements. The amusement park industry became a race to get better and newer attractions, but bereft of its zealous workforce, Eden Springs was left to survive with what it had. It was a good run, but it ended for good in 1973. The population of Benton Harbor has been trapped in a downward spiral ever since.

Do you blame the fanatical religious leader who brought the tourists to Benton Harbor in the first place, then snapped the backbone of the commune with his own moral failures? Do you blame a local government that spent its energy investing in manufacturing, believing fully that the bearded weirdos had tourism under control? Or do you blame the C-suite executives in corporate high rises who made a thousand bad decisions that ended with the shuttering of factories across Michigan and across the nation?

By the 1970s, Benton Harbor was dealing with a lot. Its dying park was finally dead. Its manufacturing industry was facing stiff overseas competition even while the city still choked on the noise and pollution of its dwindling factories. Decades of redlining practices had pushed African Americans into the homes in the shadows of those factories. By the 1980s, when the jobs started to leave Benton Harbor, whatever little value was in those homes evaporated altogether. The people in Benton Harbor were stuck there and maybe they have been ever since. If the guy with the pull cord motorbike can't get his whip going again, his predicament might be a literal one. Probably it already is.

As of the year 2000, Benton Harbor had the lowest per capita income of all the cities of Michigan. In a state with a long list of failing jurisdictions, Benton Harbor was at the bottom. Until 2023, they had more lead in their water than Flint. The water was

100

better in St. Joseph, because of course it was. The cities have separate water treatment plants, but they share a wastewater facility. The stuff they're drinking is very different, but the shit all goes to the same place.

CHAPTER ELEVEN
GOLDEN BEAR, BURIED TREASURE, AND THE RICHEST MAN IN AMERICA

The bike ride north of Benton Harbor couldn't be more peaceful, at least once we get fully north of the city. We pedal past the Jack Nicklaus designed Harbor Shores Golf Club, a place where the 70-year-old Golden Bear once sank one of the longest putts in the history of sports without even bothering to line it up.

You've seen the video, and if you haven't, you should. Nicklaus is in Benton Harbor to celebrate the opening of his course at the Change Golf Challenge. He's part of a foursome with Arnold Palmer, Tom Watson, and Johnny Miller. Miller's the one staring down a 100-foot putt on the lumpy, humpy green, lamenting that it can't be done.

Nicklaus ribs his old friend right back, telling him he just needs to make a good putt. Miller shakes his head, and Nicklaus asks a fateful question:

"Want me to show you how to putt it?"

Miller dares Nicklaus to do it, and the 18-time major winner accepts the dare, dropping a ball in Miller's spot, hastily studying the green, and barely setting his feet. It takes almost a half-swing to clear the massive green, but Nicklaus's caddy is waiting at the flag, almost like he expects to need to pull the stick.

He does need to pull the stick. The ball bounces off the back of the cup and settles into the hole as the gallery explodes. Poor Johnny Miller can only smile and shake his head. Jack Nicklaus just kicked his ass again.

On our bikes, at a pretty decent speed, it would take us four seconds to clear the length of the putt. It takes much longer to clear the golf course and everything that comes with it, but when we do, we're into the outskirts of Benton Harbor, a place that feels a lot like the outskirts of Detroit. Except this time, instead of giving way to the well-manicured suburbs of the city's elite, the weeded streets will release us into another landscape of shaded woods dotted with lakeshore views.

It's like this for hours, bike paths and quiet roads, sunshine and shade in equal measure, arriving exactly when we need them the most. Even the stretch along the backside of the abandoned nuclear power plant is scenic, despite the signs warning that we will be shot without question if we try to intrude upon the grounds. By the next October, the reactor should be resurrected, and the plant will be back online again, the first such power station to be recommissioned by federal regulators. Once it's back up again, the Palisades Power Plant will provide enough energy to power nearly a million homes.

After that, we spend an inordinate amount of time trying and failing to find a town that is ironically named Covert. And then, in a surprising instant, we've traded an idyllic cycling euphoria for another tourist town on Michigan's long tourist coast. This one is South Haven, a lake town that comes with a beautiful name, but holds an even better one in its forgotten past.

The land where the Black River spills into Lake Michigan used to be called *Ni-Ko-Nong*, an Ojibwe phrase meaning "beautiful sunset." It was true then and it's true now. Sunsets at South Haven are an event that draw an audience almost every night of the year. Tourists and locals alike flock to the shoreline to spread blankets on beaches or to seek the best park benches to watch the sun dip beyond the horizon. They'll gasp at a skyscape bathed in pinks and oranges, sometimes streaked with silvery clouds, always mirrored

104

and doubled in the ripples of the crystal blue lake. Sometimes there's applause. Often, there are tears.

That same sun set in this same place over Liberty Hyde Bailey, father of modern horticulturalism, born in South Haven in 1858. It set over James David Carrothers, author of *The Black Cat Club*; and it set over Audrey Niffenegger, author of *The Time Traveler's Wife*. In 1890 it set over the largest cannery in the world.

The South Haven sun set over Stanley Johnston, known as the *Picasso of Peaches*. His Redhaven variety is the most widely planted peach in the world, and it's named after the legendary sunsets he grew up with.

The South Haven sun has set over a handful of tragic maritime disasters, onlookers from the shore cheering a pastel skyscape, unaware that men were losing their lives just beyond the horizon that was swallowing the star of the show. For a while, that same eternal sun set over an ambitious child who would go onto become the richest man in America.

*   *   *

Daniel Ludwig was born in South Haven in 1897, a boy in a long line of sailors. Ludwig's grandparents and uncles had been captains of Great Lakes shipping vessels, and little Danny was determined to join them. Young Ludwig salvaged a 26-foot boat when he was not yet ten years old and dropped out of school in the eighth grade to begin a career in maritime shipping that would last the better part of a century.

Ludwig was just 17 when World War I began, and so, while thousands of other experienced sailors signed up to serve in the Navy, Ludwig was left behind, still too young to serve. It was exactly the stroke of luck the entrepreneurial Ludwig needed. He stepped into a sudden vacuum, establishing his own freighter business, and moving lumber and molasses around the Great Lakes. If you believe the rumors, he might have been sneaking liquor along the way as well. Ten years later, he owned more than 60 vessels and ran one of America's largest shipping companies. By the outset of World War II, Ludwig owned the shipyards that made America's boats. It was only the beginning of his wealth.

Daniel Ludwig was not content to sit on his riches, investing in a collection of luxury hotels, founding what would become the largest salt company in the world, and establishing the largest orange tree grove on the planet. In 1982, Forbes called him the richest man in America. Ludwig was famously reclusive, only ever granting one interview during his long life. He's easily the most obscure figure on the list of the richest Americans. Ludwig died in 1992 at the age of 95. No one ever had the chance to ask him if his wealth had ever bought him anything better than a South Haven sunset.

*   *   *

There's a rhyme and reason for the rhythm of the lake towns that appear on the western shores of Michigan. Wherever there's an aquatic outlet to the lake, there's a town. Generally, the bigger the outlet, the bigger the town. There was the Black River at South Haven, the Paw Paw at Benton Harbor, and the St. Joseph at St. Joseph. Before all of that, there was the Galien River way back at New Buffalo.

At Saugatuck, it's the Kalamazoo River. The town makes no effort to hide the beginnings of its history. The word Saugatuck literally means "stream outlet" in tribal tongues. William Butler

106

receives the credit as the first white man who settled the first iteration of the town all the way back in 1930, but the truth is that Saugatuck isn't really a place that was built by a man.

It was built by geography.

It's at Saugatuck where the Kalamazoo River opens up wide enough to form an inland lake and ideal harbor for ships and shipping magnates. The Kalamazoo Lake makes for peaceful waters even when Lake Michigan rages with winter storms. It's a safe place for sailors and merchandise to wait for calmer waters off the shore. In fact, it might have made more sense to call this community South Haven instead of the town just 20 miles to the south. The natural, quiet, inland harbor at Saugatuck is the southernmost such phenomenon in all of Michigan.

But I suppose Saugatuck isn't a bad name either. Butler established the place as a trading hub, establishing contact with Native Americans and bartering his whisky for their animal furs. It's a long tradition that I unknowingly participated in when I put away an old-fashioned at one of Saugatuck's signature restaurants, a place called The Butler.

It was a good old-fashioned.

Anyway, Butler's trade business was quickly eclipsed by shipping and boatbuilding. Large quantities of flour came down the Kalamazoo where boats could launch into Lake Michigan toward markets in Chicago and Milwaukee. Early lumber barons had eyes on Saugatuck, then the easiest and safest way to quickly get felled Michigan trees into the hands of Chicago builders.

When all that business dried up into the 1900s, Saugatuck made the same pivot that dozens of other stream outlets made throughout the state. It became a tourist town, first as a haven for the gay community in the 1950s and then as fourth coolest town in

America according to *Budget Travel*. Saugatuck is filled to the brim with art galleries, bookstores, coffee shops, restaurants, kitschy shops selling chicken statues, hip bars, and most of all, tourists. Thousands of them line the streets, spilling from one door and into another. It's a twenty-minute wait to get an ice cream, two hours to get seated for dinner even at 3:00 in the afternoon. More than two million people visit Saugatuck every single year, and yes, that's an awful lot for a town with a permanent population of 865.

But just barely north of Saugatuck, on the other side of the Kalamazoo River, there might be an even more impressive treasure, and like all the best treasures, this one is buried.

*   *   *

The trip from Saugatuck to Singapore isn't quite what you would expect. You skateboard your bike through the syrupy foot traffic of Saugatuck until you find yourself on the other side, by the houses, where the people live. Then it's onto a narrow road beneath a serene canopy of trees, and a harrowing cruise on narrow tires through a sandswept parking lot. From there, it's not more than a handful of dune climbs and coastal hiking before you find yourself in the town of Singapore, Michigan.

You'll quickly discover that it's nothing like Saugatuck.

That's because Singapore's not there anymore; but then, it's not exactly gone either. You just need your imagination to see it.

Founded in 1836 and imagined as a port town that would rival places such as Milwaukee and Chicago, Singapore sat on the northside of that same safe harbor that built Saugatuck, founded at the place where the brown, muddy waters of the Kalamazoo River flow reluctantly into the crystal blue of Lake Michigan. Today, a pair of disused and unimpressive lighthouses guard the spot where the two waters become one, and from the spillway pier, one can look upon the whole of the acreage that left land speculators seeing dollar signs nearly 200 years ago.

Singapore had everything a burgeoning town could want – easy access to Lake Michigan, a dammable waterway, plentiful game, pleasant temperatures, rich soil, and soaring hardwood forests that could make a man a fortune. Within just a few years of its founding, Singapore had a pair of banks, a general store, a hotel, and a schoolhouse. Each of those buildings is still out there, somewhere.

The prosperity dreamed up by the speculators was not an illusion. By 1850, Singapore had a three-masted schooner that could transport timber to Chicago, and the most powerful men in town were the lumber magnates who could take advantage of it. By 1870, several hundred people were living in Singapore, mostly employed in shipping, port management, or timber harvesting.

It could have been like this forever, and if it had been, maybe our visit to Singapore wouldn't have needed to be an imaginary one.

Except in 1871, Chicago burned down, and all over the United States, for several decades, a hundred thousand dominoes began to fall. Singapore was just one of those dominoes, but there's no need to blame Mrs. O'Leary's cow for this one. Instead, the blame lies with the people who made the decisions that came next.

As laborers and capitalists scrambled to seize the opportunity to rebuild Chicago, the timber managers in Singapore smelled the very same opportunity, and it smelled like money. A lot of money. Make no mistake. It wasn't misguided benevolence that caused everything that happened next. It was the purest and most selfish form of capitalism.

Lumber prices soared to record highs in the wake of the Great Chicago Fire, a natural consequence of the universal laws of supply and demand. Eager to make their money while they could, the people in charge of things in Singapore decided to raze an entire forest and ship it to Chicago. Those trees were processed and milled and turned into homes and churches and banks. In the end, Chicago recovered from the fire.

Singapore never would.

Bereft of the flora that once sat between their town and beach front, sand began to blow further inland as western winds whipped across Lake Michigan. It wasn't a slow encroachment either. Within four years, every pinewood cabin, every cedar-built steeple, and every oaken boatworks was swept up and buried beneath 50-foot dunes.

The Lorax's prophecy had become Flaubert's nightmare. Inevitably, at least in Singapore, sand conquers all. If the stories are to be believed, one man was more stubborn than the rest, refusing to leave the town and daily entering and exiting his home from a second story window until at last his house was swallowed up by a nature hungry to reclaim its wood. And then it was all gone.

Today, haphazard dune grasses wave in the wind above the place that used to be Singapore. A few mangy trees attempt to stake a claim to the land that used to be theirs. Sandy verbenas sparkle like amethysts in memoriam or ignorance of the town that used to be.

There is some debate about whether the decision makers in Singapore knew what they were doing. By 1870, people knew how sand dunes formed. Was it ignorance that bade them ignore the science of basic geology? Or was it greed? Did they destroy their town because they were foolish? Or was it a calculated loss, a permanent end traded for a temporary profit?

110

Today's bike ride was scheduled to end in Singapore, but of course, there's nowhere to end it, not unless we want to start digging. We'll have to retrace our steps and maybe order another old fashioned at The Butler, so long as we're willing to wait two more hours to get one.

CHAPTER TWELVE

MICHIGAN'S NEW FRONTIER

Two decades before pioneers began traversing the Oregon Trail, the fresh and wild American frontier was probably somewhere in western Michigan. With wide open spaces, irresistible lake views, mineral-rich soils, and exploitable waterways, the Wolverine state checked a lot of boxes for enterprising agriculturalists and industrial entrepreneurs. For men hungry for adventure, it checked several more. It was wild. It was free. It was largely unexplored.

There was a lot of confusion about what was out there when white men wandered west beyond the banks of the Huron. There were thick woodlands. Bears too. Native Americans. There was another great, domineering lake somewhere beyond those wild lands, but the location of that giant lake had made a mystery for mapmakers. Remember, the entire Toledo War was fought based on uncertainties about where Lake Michigan actually was.

An 1817 map of Indiana – drawn a full year *after* the Hoosiers earned their statehood – missed the location of Lake Michigan by a full 60 miles. The uncertainty about the exact dimensions and whereabouts of Michigan's hinterlands made it difficult to attract settlers, to draw up anything like county lines, and to establish the regional land offices a government needed to begin parceling its acreage.

It was an obvious problem. In order to invite people to settle its lands, Michigan was going to need to develop a better idea of where those lands were. And in order to do that, they were going to need money, equipment, supplies, scientists, guides, and a small army of security professionals to keep everyone safe.

The year was 1820. They were about to have an expedition.

Under the authority of Secretary of War John C. Calhoun, Michigan's territorial governor Lewis Cass assembled a team of 40 scientists, soldiers, and Native American guides. They were tasked with surveying and cataloging the whole of the Michigan territory, venturing all the way to Lake Michigan, and searching out the source of the Mississippi River on the other side. It was America's most ambitious exploration mission since the nation had secured its freedom. The Lewis Cass Expedition was Manifest Destiny with feet and guns.

The mission was a success. They mapped the peninsula and catalogued thousands of native plants, animals, and minerals. They took censuses of tribal nations and discovered there were more of those original inhabitants than they'd expected. They properly located Lake Michigan, and they made their way to its other side.

Cass and his men never did make their way to the source of the Mississippi River, but they did explore new parts of it. Anyway, as far as Cass was concerned, that was never the most important part. By the time he returned to Detroit, Michigan had a shape, its western shore had been mapped, and it was ready to receive settlement. The mission's geologist, Henry Rowe Schoolcraft, was appointed as Indian agent of the Michigan territory and began negotiating the treaties that would allow for the safe habitation of white people in the places they'd never been before.

Schoolcraft also took it upon himself to begin drawing lines and providing names for many of Michigan's counties. He named a few after the local tribal chiefs who'd been there when his expedition passed through, and he named another handful more after the tribes that those chiefs had been a part of.

But Michigan was a big place, and there were plenty more counties to go. That's why Schoolcraft set to the strange strategy of combining different syllables from several different tribal languages to create brand new words that *sounded* native and meant nothing. In one of the most glaring examples of native erasure, the counties honoring tribal chiefs were later renamed and whitewashed. The counties remembering Schoolcraft's nonsense words were allowed to remain.

We're in one of those jurisdictions now, chasing a tailwind north through Allegan County. Tribal linguists spent some amount of time trying to figure out what the beautiful word *Allegan* referred to. You can imagine their disappointment when they realized it meant nothing at all.

In the 1830s, Allegan County was a part of America's freshest and newest frontier, inviting pioneers and refugees to settle virgin land, put down roots, and start decorating their yards with chicken statues. In this case, we're talking about an eight-foot-tall, majestic rooster about eight miles south of Holland.

It wasn't exactly the California gold rush, but the opening of Michigan's western shores incited a scramble for the best parts of its land. It's an enormously long shoreline, with at least 450 miles of beachfront between New Buffalo and Mackinaw City, and God knows it's going to take us long enough to cycle from one end to the other. It might have seemed that there was more than enough land to go around, but the truth is that not every mile of its majestic shoreline was created equal.

There are exactly twenty places where natural and exploitable waterways spill into Lake Michigan, and the further north you go, the colder it gets and the quicker it gets that way. The best places were never going to last for long. By the 1820s, the race for the shoreline was on.

Lake towns were founded by religious separatists, ethnic refugees, and ambitious city-building entrepreneurs. It was this last group that experienced the most difficulty, and it had nothing to do with the inhospitality of the lake that provided their home.

The most ambitious profit-seekers were in the business of fur trading, and they came to the shore to set up the kinds of trading posts that had made John Jacob Astor the wealthiest man in the early United States. The only problem was that this new wave of traders was too late. Tastes had changed among European elites. American furs were no longer the haute couture they'd once been. Besides that, there were problems with overhunting in the most fruitful fur-bearing regions. It was harder to find the animals, and Native American trappers were being forced out of those lands anyway. The fur trade was facing a supply problem and a demand problem that would force a quick demise for the entire industry. Every one of those fur-trading communities failed, and in the wake of those failures, Michigan's west coast was left filled with the kinds of places that had never been exclusively profit-driven.

*   *   *

Word of Michigan's new frontier spilled into Europe, reaching all the way to a set of Dutch Calvinist pilgrims located at Zeeland, in the Netherlands. More than 200 years after Plymouth Rock, this new set of faithful believers pointed themselves to Michigan's sunset coast in order to escape religious persecution back home. The Dutch pilgrims were escaping a progressive new world order that they didn't agree with, one that included evils like science, vaccinations, and contraception.

116

Upon arriving in Michigan, they established a pair of settlements near the lake at Holland and Zeeland, one place named after the country they'd left, and another after their hometown. Like their pilgrim precursors, the Calvinists also fell into the good graces of friendly native peoples who helped them survive their first winter.

Today's Holland is a kind of Calvinist capital of the United States, and there's still plenty of Dutch there too, even besides the tulips and the tourist destinations. At least three United States ambassadors to the Netherlands have come from Holland.

But it hasn't always been easy.

During the drought of 1871, Holland burned at the same time and on the same day as Chicago's great conflagration. Wild stories abounded throughout the region, including a tale that told that an ember from the Chicago fire had ridden a wind current 100 miles due northeast across a famously wet Lake Michigan before igniting Holland. In this way, maybe it was the Hollanders who were first to call Chicago the Windy City.

Amazingly, this theory is one of the less ridiculous ones. Another oft-repeated legend claims that burning balls of methane cast off by a passing comet had lit up the young Dutch community, an awfully scientific explanation from a group of people who were willful Luddites about the Method.

Either way, on October 9, 1871, everything wooden in Holland crackled and burned, something that might have been especially difficult for the Dutch Calvinists, since that list probably included their shoes. Amazingly, only one person died.

The rebuilding of the city was tragically slow. It became apparent immediately that rebuilding Chicago was a priority and that rebuilding the other torched towns wasn't. The people of Holland had largely been saved from the flame, but in the aftermath of the

117

blaze, they were faced with starvation. Hundreds of families had been suddenly made homeless, and now they were left to stare down a winter that was already on its way. Holland had been imagined as a kind of Dutch Christian collective, a place where the people of the community would happily provide for one another in time of need. But now, there wasn't even anything left to provide.

The aftermath of the fire might have proved deadlier than the event itself but for the surprising generosity of its neighbors up shore. The people of Grand Haven arranged to send food, clothes, and whatever else the people of Holland needed to make ends meet. The Dutch pilgrims might have left the Netherlands in order to establish a separatist society, but it didn't take long for them to know and appreciate their neighbors.

We're headed now to meet those neighbors, still chasing that tailwind, cruising paved bike paths that look over occasional lakefront views, another town creeping into view every time another body of water spills into the Michigan. There's Port Sheldon on Pigeon Creek, and then, beyond the inviting roadside sign that bids you to enter into Michigan's Rosy Mound, there's Grand Haven, situated on the Grand River.

The Grand River is its own curiosity, carving a wandering kind of drunk man's path through lower Michigan, touching parts of Jackson, Lansing, and Grand Rapids before spilling into the lake at the end of its meandering. As for Grand Haven, it's another of Michigan's geographic miracles, kissed by the kinds of natural harbors that made it a logical place to become Coast Guard City, USA. The designation was officially bestowed by Congress in 1998.

The population of Grand Haven is barely 10,000, but during its annual Coast Guard Festival, that number balloons significantly. More than 350,000 people pour into the small town at the end of each July to throw a party that is, on all sides, surrounded by apocalyptic traffic. During the Coast Guard Festival, a cyclist can get from one side of town to the other a full hour faster than a car, a distance of less than two-and-a-half miles.

Michigan's lake towns are certainly not monolithic in their histories or presents, but many of them have trod a similar journey. They were born as villages platted by a visionary whose dream very rarely came true. Then came the lumber barons, flush with cash and bravado, each making a series of rich promises that lasted right up until the last tree was felled. That's when the ephemeral Timber Daddy moved onto the next town, and in Grand Haven's case, nobody bothered to tell the guy that he'd missed a spot.

I do not know nearly enough about trees to describe to you what I saw as we pedaled past Grand Haven's Duncan Park, but I recognized it immediately, without ever knowing I should have been looking for it. This wasn't just a slice of old forest. It was an ancient one, a tiny sliver of the last remaining virgin woodlands on Michigan's lower peninsula.

There was the way the sunlight dappled in the dangling branches of hundred-year hemlocks, each limb the arm of a Christmas tree weighed down by too many ornaments. Hemlocks are the kinds of sturdy, hearty trees that used to rule over this part of Michigan, immune to all matter of hardships, except for pollution, which it is especially vulnerable to. The hemlock is a tree that does not thrive in a man-made world, nor is it a tree that is of any special use to the men who make the world.

And yet, it was not the hemlocks that whispered of the great age of these woods. It was not either the soaring beeches, the maple trees, or the red oaks.

Instead, it was the presence of death, fully unscheduled. It was the presence of a death not hastened, not interrupted, and only barely observed. It was the fallen branches, the limbs of the grey trees yet to leaf even though we were well into a warm and wet summer as we rode through the place.

There is a lot that differentiates a proper old-growth forest, but maybe not more than this: Duncan Park is one of the only places remaining where the trees are allowed to die of natural causes. They're not cut down when they're mature enough for paper pulp. They're not pruned when their branches rub against the gutters of some house. They die when they die, and then they rot, unmolested by human hands or human agendas.

And then, just like an abandoned Michigan logging town, life has a way of springing forth from those dying places. It might not be what's expected, and it almost certainly won't be what it was before. It might not feel like a rebirth that comes from the neat order of a planner's careful hand. Bugs and mushrooms crawl over leveled limbs, softening and returning them to the earth as nutrients and soil. From somewhere inside that deathly mush, a seed sprouts and wiggles its way toward a sunny spot in the canopy, a shining treetop gap only recently made vacant. The black-barked tree will sprout a cherry and its fruit will be delicious.

It's a Michigan story if there ever was one.

More than a century after the fur traders failed and the lumber barons skipped town, more than a quarter-million people will crowd into Grand Haven's downtown to sample beer, eat tacos, enjoy carnival rides, and sing along with the Jimmy Buffett cover band, Parrots of the Caribbean.

I'm just glad we'll be safely through the traffic before the festivities begin.

CHAPTER THIRTEEN

THE BENEVOLENT RULE OF MICHIGAN'S LUMBER BARONS

The infinite blue of North America's Great Lakes has given rise to a host of the continent's most impressive metros. To name a few: Buffalo, Cleveland, Toledo, Detroit, Toronto, Chicago, Milwaukee. You already figured out that none of these are located in western Michigan.

Perhaps this isn't so surprising, especially given the business interests of the first speculators to alight upon the shoreline. The fur traders were here for a good time, not a long time. Gilded Age lumber barons were never known as the kinds of people who were concerned about the long-term future of anything, except maybe their bank accounts.

So, Illinois gets Chicago, Ohio gets Cleveland, and New York gets Buffalo. Even Duluth, Minnesota has a population more than double the largest city on Michigan's sunset coast: Muskegon.

That's where we are now, and if you're looking to get started as a cycling-tourist-historian, this is where you should begin your journey. We'll spend the next several hours surrounded by ideal scenery beneath shade trees while cruising the smoothest bike paths I've ever seen.

At least that's what we'll be doing as soon as we can figure out how to get out of Muskegon. So far, that's proving a bit of a challenge, although it's probably more my fault than Muskegon's.

Muskegon's story goes a lot like the other towns we've travelled through during the past several days. Centuries of Native Americans, a few decades of fur traders, and then a lumber baron intent on stripping the land and then leaving for greener pastures.

121

But Muskegon's lumber baron never left. In fact, he's still there, at least in statue form, taking a seat on a bench in downtown Muskegon. You can sit with him for a spell if you'd like to.

Charles Hackley came to Muskegon in 1856, making his earliest money carving some of western Michigan's earliest roadways and then investing that money into the thickest, most valuable forested acres he could get his hands on. The lumber baron's playbook was markedly simple, and Hackley followed the plan *almost* exactly.

Step One: Acquire good logging land.

Step Two: Lease logging rights to the land, charging individuals by the day or by the hour for the right to fell your trees. You can even cut a few down yourself if you want to, but this isn't necessary. What you really need to do now is to save money aggressively until…

Step Three: Build your own sawmill. This guarantees that your trees will be processed in priority and at the best prices and also allows you to make money off of trees felled in other forests, even the ones you don't own. You already know what you're going to use that money for.

Step Four: Buy up more forest, preferably every acre of loggable land for which your sawmill is the most convenient processing facility.

Step Five: *(Optional)* Start your own freight business so that you control the product from beginning to end.

Step Six: Once a grid is completely cleared, sell the land to a farmer for more than it cost you in the first place.

Step Seven: Once all of the forest is gone, move to the Pacific
               Northwest with your capital. Rinse and repeat.

Hackley wasn't the first lumber baron to call Muskegon his home, but he was the last one, and he was its biggest. By the 1880s, the entire city was built around the processing of trees. There were *at least* 47 active sawmills around Muskegon Lake. Hackley's firm alone processed more than 30,000,000 feet of lumber per year during the decade.

But by the end of the 1880s, the forests were almost gone. The lumber men who had been Hackley's competitors were out of town, seeking new forests in new places, building sawmills on rivers only recently discovered. Hackley stayed back, not shuttering his mill until the last pine tree in the region was processed in 1894.

Hackley might not have been aware of the environmental disaster he'd wrought, but he couldn't miss the economic devastation that was about to come upon the city that he called his home. Muskegon had become known as "The Lumber Queen of the World," and now it had no trees. Muskegon had a population of 20,000. Most of them were employed as tree cutters or tree processors or tree shippers. The ones who weren't in the tree business were employed to feed, clothe, lodge, and entertain the ones who were. It had taken less than thirty years to erase Muskegon's forests. It would be a lot quicker to erase its city.

By 1891, Muskegon was on fire, neither from drought, nor airborne embers, nor methane fireballs from nearby comets. The cause of this one was probably arson, an out-of-work sawmill owner trying to recoup just a little bit of insurance money to feed his family.

This is when Hackley deviated from the playbook, skipping Step Seven altogether and trying something different instead. That's because, right at the moment when every proper lumber baron was supposed to pack up and leave town, Hackley didn't.

He stayed.

Charles Hackley had a conscience in the part of his brain where other lumber barons only had profit motive. Recognizing that his city was literally going to burn itself to the ground, Hackley invested a third of his massive net worth into reinvigorating Muskegon. He built a library, an art gallery, a park, and a hospital. He invested heavily into schools and endowments, monuments, statues, and providing for the poor. After a $12 million gift, Muskegon briefly considered changing its name to Hackleyville.

Hackley's investment in Muskegon went beyond even his philanthropic efforts. Recognizing that the people of the city needed jobs even more than they needed libraries, Hackley spent the second half of his career soliciting investment in the city. He convinced companies like Brunswick, Central Paper, and Continental Motors to open up in Muskegon.

None of this exculpates Hackley's desecration of the local environment, but it is a credit to the man that he didn't take his blocks and leave when the lumber industry fully consumed itself. Instead, he stacked them strategically, setting the table for the continuation of a city on the brink. Today's Muskegon remains a sounding echo of the groundwork that Hackley laid behind him.

It's lucky for the nation that Hackley guaranteed a thriving Muskegon before his death in 1905. Muskegon gave rise to Buster Keaton and Iggy Pop. The Santa Claus that you recognize today was drawn by the pencil of Haddon Sundblom, a Swedish immigrant who came of age in Hackley's Muskegon. During the 1960s, Muskegon was even responsible for a pair of Miss Americas.

And just in case this chapter has persuaded you to think that selfish lumber barons represent the grossest possible manifestation of profit-minded exploitation, I should also tell you that Muskegon is the birthplace of televangelist (and convicted felon) Jim Bakker.

The echoes of Hackley's influence are still felt throughout Muskegon today, more than a century after the man's death. At least two of the companies that he brought to the city during the timber twilight remain in business. His name is still on the library, the hospital, the middle school, the football stadium, and a park. His stately Victorian home remains open for tours, and the house's 13-color exterior paint scheme shines like a lighthouse in an otherwise quaint and understated Michigan neighborhood. In short, you can't miss the guy, no matter how hard you try.

Hackley, of course, was not the only wealthy baron in these parts. As we roll north of Muskegon toward the town of Whitehall, we find ourselves squarely in another lumber fiefdom, this one the dominion of a New Englander named Charles Mears.

The bike ride through the land that might have once been the Kingdom of Mears is smooth enough, skirting neatly scheduled forests replanted in gridded man-made rows. It's as serene as a bike ride can be, save for the occasional echoes of the blood curdling screams in the distance.

It's a pretty surprising thing to happen upon an amusement park in the middle of nowhere, somewhere north of a city that's not that big and somewhere south of a town that's a heck of a lot smaller. I'm pretty sure the screams came from a ride called the Shivering Timbers, a wooden roller coaster that covers a full mile in two-and-a-half minutes. With the tailwind, we're just about able to make the same time, but our ride is much smoother.

Anyway, soon enough we're into Whitehall, cruising adorable downtown streets and an interurban bike trail. We cycle past a whitewashed public art wall, a well-intended project that was quickly abandoned when local hoodlums started – probably unsurprisingly – drawing dicks all over the thing.

It feels like we've left Whitehall just as soon as we've arrived, but it's going to be a lot longer before we leave behind the duchy lands of Charles Mears. His was a kind of colonial expansion. Before the day is over, we'll ride through several of the towns that Mears helped to create, at least the ones that are still standing.

Charles Mears began his lumber empire in 1840 at Whitehall, following the lumber baron's playbook exactly. He purchased loggable land. He built a sawmill. He carved a channel to the lake. He platted a town, and he named it after himself. This place used to be known as Mears, Michigan several years before it was Whitehall.

By 1854, the forests were already beyond their peak production and Mears journeyed into the north, looking for new places to plant his flag. He followed the same route that we're tracing today, basking in sunshine and freshwater spray, soaring golden sand dunes marking the only acres the timbermen wouldn't be able to cut down.

Eventually, Mears made his way to Pentwater and so did we. It's a region that is now a part of the Asparagus Capital of the World, but that's not what it was when Mears and his men arrived in 1855. Back then it was all soaring, virgin, hardwood forest. Mears knew what to do. He followed all the same steps in the same order, but by now he'd learned some of the efficiencies he didn't know before. This time it took less than five years before he emptied the land of its canopy. Already it was time to move to a new place. The life of a lumber baron is as transient as it is lonely.

Charles Mears made his last major stop in Ludington, putting his skills to use in service of the already-established timber kings of the region. Mears didn't fell any trees in the town, but he did carve its channel.

The marriage of Pere Marquette Lake and Lake Michigan is probably Charles Mears' piece de resistance. It's a grand deep waterway with a wide channel that guaranteed the delivery of larger lumber loads than any of his previous works. Even after the timber trade ended, Ludington would remain a primary shipping port for decades to come. Today's US-10 still connects Wisconsin to Michigan via a 60-mile ferry trip that runs daily from Ludington between May and October.

Maybe it could be said that the lumber barons giveth and the lumber barons taketh away, but that's a pretty generous description of a playbook that's rooted in taking as much as you can without ever giving anything back. This section of Michigan, lined with all the lush and living miles between Muskegon and Ludington, is the exception to that rule.

Later in his life, Charles Mears became a patron of the region that had filled his own coffers with such obscene wealth. He platted the new town of Mears after Whitehall removed his name from its signs. He founded the town of Hamlin, only to watch it wash away after a dam failure. That failed venture would eventually become Ludington State Park. He donated the land that would become Mears State Park. His daughter donated the land that would become Silver Lake State Park.

*   *   *

It's the end of the most beautiful bike ride we've had so far, 72 sunkissed, sandstrewn miles brought to us, in part, by the benevolent lumber barons of western Michigan. In Michigan's long history, there are more stories like these than you'd probably expect, but don't be fooled into believing that men like these were the norm. There were plenty more who followed the playbook all the way to its miserable end, but the towns they founded didn't put statues of those men on their benches. More often than not, those towns didn't even survive to tell the tale. Imagine a tycoon eviscerating a region's natural resources for profit, then taking the money to the other side of the country, and you've got a pretty good proxy for understanding what happened to Michigan's irreplaceable forests.

Mears and Hackley are not blameless here. They're just as responsible as the least scrupulous woodmen for the desecration of those forests. The loss of those environments is something that cannot be repaid through any amount of philanthropy.

And yet, it is true that if Mears and Hackley hadn't razed the woodlands, it would have certainly been someone else, and those someones might not have given anything back to the people and places they'd plundered.

In 1820, Michigan was the home to the richest and most valuable woodlands in the known United States. Eighty years later, most of the trees were gone. It's strange that building a state requires so much irreversible destruction. It's strange that so much of Michigan's early economy was built around wealthy out-of-towners who came to cut, chop, and leave. It's strange that so many of its early towns were centered around industries that were so decidedly impermanent in nature.

But given the unfettered and unregulated capitalism of the time, maybe the strangest bit of all is that there were barons who didn't always act like them. Maybe the strangest part is that some of the people who worked as Professional Destroyers of Lands actually took the time to build something instead. They wiped out a lot of beauty when they came through with their axes and saws, but it's not hard to imagine that it could have been a lot worse.

CHAPTER FOURTEEN
WHERE THE NORTH BEGINS

There's a certain cosmopolitan flavor that comes with the Michigan towns that dot the southern shores of Lake Michigan. There's a taste of something refined, something urban, and something not quite Michigan. There's the sound of Chicago's stretched vowels and clipped words, the rushed cadence of summer tourists trying to live an unhurried life without really knowing how. It's a feeling wafted and whispered along friendly south winds, but the winds have dwindled with every new northern mile and so have the fading voices of faraway cities.

But the echoes of those voices are not quite gone yet, at least not as we cycle north from Ludington. There's a lingering aroma left behind by touristy travelers who tamed towns they once loved wild. By the end of the day, that smell will be a forgotten memory. Today's bike ride is Michigan unadulterated, maybe the most authentic expression of the state. I'm convinced that this is what Tim Allen was whispering about when he described *Pure Michigan*. Everything about the world is going to change in the most marvelous ways during the next 70 miles, because depending on who you ask, we will have finally arrived in The North.

It's a point of some contention where the actual North of Michigan begins. Yoopers would tell you it doesn't happen until you cross the bridge and leave the southern peninsula altogether. Others will tell you that northern Michigan *begins* at Grand Rapids. The distance between those two places is more than 200 miles and there's lots of wiggle room for lots of divergent opinions in between.

The state of Michigan has wisely stayed out of the debate, but at least one of its counties has waded boldly into the discussion. Clare County is a landlocked place in the center of the mitten, a tiny inland jurisdiction that we've never even seen before. Its county seat has fewer than 2,500 inhabitants, and the city of Clare is not even fully contained in the county that carries its name.

This same Clare County is the one that calls itself "The Gateway to the North", and for my part, I'm inclined to agree with the assessment. A horizontal line drawn from the geographic center of Clare County intersects Lake Michigan just about a mile north of Ludington, and that's where we're pedaling now, another exquisite route in a long line of them, but the first one in a while where everything feels *different*.

That's not to say that the bike ride is without its difficulties. It's not raining when we begin the ride, but it's not *not* raining either. That leaves us stuck between a pair of impossible decisions. Either we wear all of our rain gear and sweat through our shirts, or we keep it stowed and leave ourselves exposed to the rain. At least that's Ashley's choice. I didn't bring any rain gear to begin with. Either way we're both going to finish this ride wet. Maybe that seems like an unpleasant guarantee, but hey, that's life in The North.

The woods here are as thick as the clouds. The roads are narrow, but they are quiet. Mailboxes mark the curbs in front of houses we cannot see. There's a lot that disappears behind those trees, entire stories unexplored. The newspaper I read this morning reported on bear sightings in the region, a development that has filled me with excitement and filled Ashley with alarm. On the long list of Pure Michigan experiences that I want to have, a spontaneous encounter with a bear is right near the top.

But if it's going to happen, it's not going to happen today. There will be no bears on this course, just telephone poles standing like sentries along the narrow road, their electrified wires pointing lines toward infinity, but more importantly toward Manistee, the city of the Spirit of the Woods.

Manistee's earliest history is not unique, at least not among the towns we've travelled during the past week or so. There were traders and there were loggers, and then the whole city burned down on the same day as Holland and Chicago. But when the city rebuilt itself from those ashes, it built up a decidedly different place than the towns to its south, and you can feel it in the architecture and the way the town chooses to hug its river and not its lake.

From the moment we arrive, I love Manistee more than any town we've seen so far. It hasn't been that long since we set off for the morning, but already I know we're going to have to stop here. I want more coffee because I always want more coffee, and anyway, it's starting to rain just a little harder than it was before. Remarkably, if there was ever one storefront in the world that could provide everything I ever needed, it's right here in Manistee.

We wait out the passing rainclouds inside The Outpost, a sporting goods store and coffee shop. They have lightweight raincoats and locally roasted small batch coffees, and I'll take one of both, please. We sip and we wait and there is no hurry here, because this is The North, and the schedule is just different. It's taken until now for me – a man literally riding a bicycle around a state – to fully realize that the fastest way is not always the best one.

None of this is to suggest that Manistee is some kind of a backwoods Yukon hinterland situated beyond some forgotten vista that progress has yet to penetrate. After all, the coffee I was drinking was a cortado, and it was a good one. Manistee is a modern town, but that does not mean it's been completely tamed. There still ring the echoes of a Michigan wild that have yet to be fully driven out, a reminder of the time when the place was the domain of lumberjacks who knew neither law nor lawyer, at least until Thomas Jefferson Ramsdell arrived.

Ramsdell's 1860 journey into Manistee was far more harrowing than our bike ride into the place. Ramsdell made the trip in the winter, which was a questionable choice to begin with, and he rode the whole way in a very literal one-horse open sleigh. There were no roads and there were hardly trails. He might have expected a frosty welcome as a young and ambitious lawyer setting up shop amidst the hard drinking lumberjacks, but that wasn't the reality he walked into. For the rough and tumble woodsmen, Ramsdell had already proved his mettle just by making the journey.

Thomas Jefferson Ramsdell would go onto become Manistee's most important founding father. He built the first bridge across the Manistee River and watched that bridge burn during the 1871 fire. He opened the first hardware store and launched the first newspaper. He opened the first bank, developed the first Water Works, and built the first school. In 1902 he built the Ramsdell Theatre. That last building is still standing, but Ramsdell himself had been dead a few decades by the time James Earl Jones began his illustrious acting career on its stage.

I want to explore all of it, but we really must be going, and Manistee does not try to hold onto you when you leave. There are not stoplights at each block, there are not the trappings of aspiring suburbs. There are only woods and lake. Our road skirts both, bending and bowing nearer and further the water, the edge of the shoulder sometimes not more than fifty feet from the murky grey waters reflecting a murky grey sky.

It's a sad moment when our route turns inland, but this is Michigan, and when you point yourself away from one lake, you're never far from the next one. We eat lunch at a gas station in Onekama, but it's a nice gas station, and it comes with a view of Portage Lake. The name of the town rolls nicely off the tongue, and it should. Onekama means *Singing Water* in the land's original language. On this grey day, the song is an elegiac tune, punctuated by the pitter patter of occasional teardrops on the milky mercury of the overcast lake. We eat apples and dill pickles and candy bars and spicy jerky made from a non-traditional kind of animal.

Then we charge back into the rain, tracing a northerly route through a set of wooded inland roads. For ten miles we don't see another person. We don't see a car. Buttressed to the left, right, and above by healthy hardwoods, we don't see much of the sky, and we certainly don't see the lake.

It's not until Arcadia that we emerge from the canopy to find a sky that's grown angrier by the minute. We pause at the beachfront to watch wind whipped waves crest out on the open water and then lap hungrily at the shore. The steely grey of the swirling lake reminds onlookers that the wet world out there is as dangerous as it is beautiful. The white spray that accompanies the breaking of each wave might well be the reflective glint of cold honed metal. Water once serene seems suddenly sinister, and maritime maps mention that even though the violent waters keep secrets in their depths, they don't always keep those secrets well.

We can see, even beneath the dully clouded sky, the remains of the wreckage of a boat called the Minnehaha. Weathered wooden planks poke curiously through the places where the receding waters have ripped away the layer of sand that used to keep the boat hull buried beneath the beach. It is not a hidden shipwreck, and it is not a new one either.

The Minnehaha ran aground in 1893.

A massive, busted piece of the ship's starboard hull washed up on the Arcadia shore a day after the wreck, and it's been there ever since, a visceral reminder that Lake Michigan has been a dangerous place to work much longer than it's been a pleasant place to play. Somewhere at the bottom of the churning water, there are the remains of the Minnehaha's payload: 58,000 bushels of corn and six unfortunate sailors. There are plenty of opinions about where The North begins, but once you hit the towns where they retain their wreckages as welcome and warning, I think you're there.

Even the shape and character of the land changes as we continue beyond Arcadia and further into The North. Like the rest of the state, this used to be covered by ice, miles wide and long and deep. Once the Ice Age ended and those glacial sheets receded, they took just a little longer making their way out of The North, carving the kinds of bluffs and valleys that you don't find downstate.

In short, this is where the hills are, and we find them over and again as we push toward the end of the day. Tired, burning legs turn labored revolutions of heavy pedals as we approach a hilltop called Inspiration Point. Maybe it was the grade of the hill and maybe it was the view from the top, but all of it has taken my breath away. I'm collapsed and quivering at a picnic bench that looks out into forever. An absent sun emerges from a break in the clouds, and the lake somehow reflects a blue that is not yet present in the sky. I was not impressed the first time I saw the ocean, because I'd already seen the lakes, and from a hundred yards out it's all the same: crashing, infinite wet as far as the eye can see.

There used to be a lot of ducks here, even more ducks than there are now. It was enough ducks that the French named the river after those ducks: *La Rivière aux Bec-scies*. It's a term that the French used specifically to reference saw billed ducks, and it's one that English speakers struggled to pronounce when they began to settle the bottom of Michigan's pinky finger. The river became the Betsie. The county became Benzie, and that's where we've been ever since we reached the apex of Inspiration Point.

We've been riding MI-22 for a while now, and we'll be on it for the better part of the next three days. But once we're into Benzie County, our road has taken on an additional name. It is now Michigan's Scenic Highway, and the name is apt. We gaze across sand dunes like mountains, golden shining sand beneath a sky growing bluer by the moment. At least in Benzie County, the rain has pattered out. Even the turning wind, now pushing back against us, couldn't ruin the last part of this ride.

When we reach the town of Elberta, it welcomes us with a diorama of chicken statues in a garden scene just within the town's limits. There are at least a dozen of the little cluckers, some dolled up in red, white, and blue top hats. We're somewhere between Memorial Day and Independence Day, and it's impossible to know if the plastic poultry parade is marching out of one holiday or into the next. We stop longer than we should and take more pictures than we ought.

As for the history of Elberta, it was far enough north that even the loggers didn't get here first. Instead, it was George Cartwright, a real estate speculator who began seizing up property and platting towns. He was rewarded for his pioneering spirit, and when the lumberjacks made their way to his region, Cartwright was more than happy to sell his land at a profit.

It was here that the Betsie River became bloated enough to be called Betsie Lake, and Cartwright recognized the boon when he saw it. He established two towns. The place that would become Elberta was on the lake's southern shores, and the place that would become the city of Frankfort was on its northern shores. Frankfort isn't too far away, and Ashley and I don't know it yet, but we are absolutely about to fall in love.

Maybe it's because this was the place where the sun finally came out after spending a dreary day in a sopping saddle. Maybe it was those same rainy conditions that scared travelers into staying indoors, leaving Frankfort feeling like a kind of booming tourist town that hadn't yet been overrun by them.

Maybe it was the way Betsie Lake skirted downtown to the south and the way Lake Michigan opened to the west, or maybe it was just our legs, still whining about the hills, excited to see the hotel and to know they were done. It's hard to say what it was, but before we'd even finished showering off a day's worth of road grime, Ashley and I were talking openly about buying a house and living here forever. That was before we found the exquisite Belgian brewery with the very accommodating gluten free menu. It was before we stumbled into the most gorgeous independent bookstore, before the walk toward the art museum on the beach. We wanted to stay here before we found the coffee shop, the one that tap danced along the line between hip and pretentious.

We loved Frankfort before we spent the night in its historic hotel, a feature of the town since 1869, before we knew that Al Capone used to control the brick house on the beach, that his elaborate tunnels snuck between the home and our hotel. According to Wikipedia, there are 1,252 people who live here, and we want to join them.

Oh, and I should also tell you this:

Frankfort, Michigan has absolutely the ugliest lighthouse I've ever seen in my life.

Listen, I do not know what sort of brutalist architect looked at every adorable lighthouse that had ever been built and then decided to put this shining sentinel up at Frankfort's North Pier. The whitewashed steel pyramid might be held together by rivets, as if it was assembled from the rejected pieces of a World War I German tank. I do not know the name of the man who designed the North Pier Lighthouse, nor do I know which eastern European prison inspired his creation. This thing is an affront to nature and aesthetics, possibly offensive to God and man, and the best part is, the people of Frankfort are fighting like hell to save it.

There are posters and flyers on benches, on telephone poles, and on every bulletin board in every community gathering place. The lighthouse needs fixing, and the Friends of the Lighthouse need support and funding to make that happen. And when they are at last finished with their noble quest, will the North Pier Lighthouse look any better than it does now?

It will not.

I wonder if the tourists who visit lighthouses are ever inspired by those shining beacons to consider their own mortality. After all, why is a lighthouse built but to warn of impending doom? And I guess when you think about it that way, maybe a lighthouse isn't supposed to be warm and cozy and inviting. Anyway, this one certainly isn't.

Lake Michigan is the deadliest of the Great Lakes for sailors and the largest graveyard for their ships. The ships that went down outside of Frankfort had names like: Jessie Scarth, Ida, Comet,

139

Westmoreland, Blackhawk, and Menekaunee. There are the skeletons of men in the water.

The North Pier Lighthouse was never imagined as the backdrop of a photograph on someone's Instagram story, and it certainly isn't going to become that now. Instead, it's a reminder of a brutal and dangerous history, the story of a people who earned their Wolverine nickname.

It would be a corruption of the facts to pretend that The North was ever wildly more dangerous than the rest of Michigan. The whole state was pretty rough there for a while. But in The North, there's no attempt at hiding it. Its lighthouses were built for the people in the water, not the people on the land. Its shipwrecks remain on the beaches *because that's where they washed up*. At Frankfort, there's no attempt to cover up the town's rough and tumble history, and the only thing they whitewash is the bottom ten feet of that lighthouse, four times, every single year. The North does not change for the tastes of the people downstate, and The North does not care if you love it.

This is The North. The North is perfect.

CHAPTER FIFTEEN
THE PINKY

There is a lot of blood on the woman, and the woman cannot tell us how it got there. She was out for a run. Training for a marathon. She thinks she might have tripped. She must have tripped. Did you hit your head? I did not hit my head. Your head is bleeding. I must have hit my head. How many fingers am I holding up? My shoulder hurts. Can you tell me how many fingers I'm holding up? My shoulder hurts very bad.

Not every unexpected surprise on a bike ride is a good one, but I suppose it was a good thing we were there when we were. Ashley is a nurse and a very good one. She knew exactly what to do.

I knew how to direct traffic.

While we waited for the EMTs to arrive, Ashley talked to the woman, kept her awake, kept her engaged. She learned a lot during those minutes. The woman was living in California. She was out here at Crystal Lake on a girls' trip. They'd been having a good time. She had that marathon to train for. She didn't know what she tripped on. Her shoulder hurt a lot.

It was some number of minutes before the woman was whisked away in the back of an ambulance. The woman wound up with a broken bone. Tests for a concussion were nonconclusive. Her marathon would have to wait another year.

The whole episode was sad and tragic, but it was also a ringing endorsement of Michigan's tourism industry. The woman was from California, after all, a place famous for its own coastal views and perfect summers. But when it came time for vacation, she chose the pinky of Michigan's Mitten, a place that is not easy to get to. It's not like there's a direct flight from Los Angeles to Crystal Lake.

And yet there she was, having the time of her life on the lakes, at least until the morning's tumble. When her vacation came to a quick and unscheduled end, the lakes would not miss her. They would not even notice. There were plenty more tourists to take her place.

In the wake of the decline of Michigan's more traditional manufacturing industries, it was a burgeoning tourism business that saved the state. Unfortunately, as we'll see throughout the Pinky, tourism may also be thing that kills it.

The problem of short-term rentals has plagued communities throughout the state, but it's a problem that's most prevalent throughout the Pinky. Walk up and down the streets of the downtowns at Empire and Glen Arbor in the summer, and you'll see plenty of people. But most of them don't live there. And the people that work in the shops? Fewer of them are living there too.

There's too much money in the Airbnb game, pricing out residents and occasionally erasing the history of charming lake towns in favor of serving the transient visitors who live there for a week. When a particularly adventurous tourist says he wants to "eat where the locals eat", his guide doesn't know what to tell him.

There aren't any locals anymore.

As for the visitors, at least it can be said they have good taste. The westside of Michigan's Pinky is home to Sleeping Bear Dunes, one of the most beautiful and breathtaking destinations in the United States. Good Morning America went so far as to call it the "Most Beautiful Place in America". More than 1.7 million people visit Sleeping Bear each year, and if that seems like a lot, it is. The closest towns to the park have a combined population of barely a thousand.

For a cyclist, Sleeping Bear is a heaven. The paved bike trail veers off from the main road at exactly the point where the main road turns to gravel. We cruise up and down spiky hills like we're riding the back of a stegosaurus, our route carving tight curves through thick wood, then opening into views of the soaring sandy hills that earned the park its name. The dunes are said to resemble the fattened belly of a great bear lying asleep on its back.

The views are as stunning as we've been told, and it's difficult to denigrate the millions of visitors who come through here when we're two of them and we're already talking about bringing the kids back. It's just wild enough up here to feel the thrust of everything that Michigan offers. Signs warn us to wear bright colors so as not to accidentally be shot by hunters who might otherwise confuse us for an elk. Different signs warn us that we are entering bear territory. I am disappointed when we don't discover one.

The bike path dumps us out into Glen Arbor, a grid of charming blocks positively invaded by visitors. The sky over the town is a dull, sullen grey, stretched tight like it might break open any minute, though it never does. The town had been put here by fishermen and lumberjacks, its narrow streets sufficient for hauling a catch or trucking the timber out of town.

But the streets are choked now, packs of tourists, laughing, staring into iPhones, hauling bags filled with trinkets, dripping ice cream into the spaces between their toes inside their pink flip-flops purchased from a gas station up the road. The sidewalks are narrow, too narrow, and the tourists walk four abreast anyway, oblivious. Cars snarl an intersection, inching forward, waiting for a break in the shoppers' parade at the crosswalk.

It's a mixed bag for the people who call the town their home, a lot of riches for four months of work if you own the ice cream shop or if you own a collection of rentable beach houses. As for everyone else, the best you're likely to hear is that the tourism is a necessary evil, but an evil nonetheless.

The place wasn't built for this, not really. Not for the noise or the crush of bodies. On this day, the weather is just unpleasant enough to keep the tourists from the beach, but not nearly so bad as to keep them inside their expensive lodgings. The town strains against the weight and force and sound. The old men shake their heads while they wait for a table at the diner off the drag, the one place that was supposed to be their quiet haven, but someone's found it and told everyone else.

"Guess we'll drink our coffee standing," says one of the men, gesturing to a waitress.

She returns, flustered, but with coffee in tow. She hands the cups off to the men, as the one in the hat offers a comment toward the harried server – "Wasn't like this before."

Her back is turned before the words leave his mouth. She doesn't have time to answer him back, didn't have time to hear him in the first place. The diner is filled with customers, and they are all excited to take pictures of their food. When someone else says aloud that their emergency services don't have the capacity to handle all of this, I don't have the heart to tell them what we saw this morning.

And then, just as soon as it started, Glen Arbor is over. Thanks to a bike lane, we've gotten through one side of town and out the other faster than the cars. Then it's back onto open roads and grey skies that have yet to make up their minds. It sprinkles as soon as we take off the rain jackets. The sun comes out as soon as they go back on again. At last, we're in Leland, another town overrun by outsiders, but one with a wholly unexpected character.

You wouldn't see it unless you wandered off of the main drag, which means that a lot of people don't see it, but there's something historic and important in Leland, just along the edge of the lake. It's protected and preserved – the Historic Fishtown of northern Michigan's proud pinky finger.

It is not a place, but the memory of a place, something alive that should not have survived, and yet it persists. The shanties lean against one another in a way that seems accidental, weathered wood blistered and grayed by decades of wind off the water. The roofs sag, but only just, like they hold their breath to keep from collapsing. The air is thick with the smell of fish, clean and sharp and briny.

They come here, too, the people, so many people, more than there should be, their voices rising and falling and breaking like waves against a hull. They move with the curiosity of outsiders, the confidence of visitors who remain convinced they have found something top-secret even though the place is teeming with people just like them. They buy the smoked fish and the T-shirts, they take pictures of the signs nailed to the doors of the shops that were once something else: a fish house, a shed, a place where the work was done, the cutting and gutting, the catching and selling.

The boardwalk groans under their weight, all of them weaving from shop to shop. Behind fenced barriers hang rusty pulleys and faded buoys that hang like ghosts from a time when Fishtown was only what its name says it was, not what it has become: a memory, a monument, a performance. The air smells of fish and money and exhaust, and it sounds like the boat motors still sputtering in the water where charter captains ferry families to the places where the water is quiet and wide and empty.

145

Believe me, if any of this is a problem, I recognize that I am a part of it. I am here, in the middle of all of it, *visiting it*, looking at it, then wandering away from it, waiting for the next stunning Michigan performance – a sunset, a fudge shoppe, a hill made out of a lot of sand. I have come to see and smell and taste and feel and hear, and I have come, just like everyone else, to trample all over it.

And then, once the trampling is complete, we're back onto the road, but then this part of the ride is different. These roads are quiet, quieter even than the bike trails we'd ridden earlier in the day. It's as if the other tourists haven't realized that there is more Michigan north of Leland, more to be discovered, and more to be consumed and devoured.

We'll stay at a proper Bed and Breakfast for the evening, and on the walk from our lodging to our dinner (at a bowling alley), we do not see anyone else on the streets and we do not see cars driving them. We stop for ice cream and the man running the shop is surprised to see us. He's somehow just opened for the season, and it is already deep into June.

Down the street from the ice cream shop, at the edge of the marina, there is a yard filled with the most insane collection of yard art – a giraffe, a rhino, a bear, a tiger, a lion, a man-sized yellow M&M, a dinosaur, a pirate ship. Remarkably, there are no chicken statues. More remarkably, there is not a parade of travelers taking selfies in front of the menagerie.

This is Northport, Michigan; and so far as I can tell, the tourists haven't found it yet. Maybe it's because the place is so far north or maybe it's the town's generic sounding name. Perhaps things would be so much different if they'd kept their original moniker – Waukazooville. It sure is more fun to say, anyway.

Northport is quaint on its own terms, not desiring to make a show of its small-town charm, nor making any attempt to fit neatly into a box of similar lake towns. After spending a week passing through dozens of shoreline communities, Northport is maybe the first place that feels like it's built more for the people who live there than the people who visit.

I love it immediately.

But then, it's not for me.

There are some attempts being made to establish Northport as a more desirable destination, and smart people have capitalized on the town's position as a kind of remote northern outpost. It's not for everyone, of course, but Northport has gained a reputation as a regional dark sky paradise. The place comes alive when the town goes dark. Unpolluted by light, the sky puts on a show after sunset and the show costs nothing to produce. They tell me that Northport was filled beyond capacity during the meteor shower, but today it is overcast. It's a Friday, and the bar is closed.

It's hard to imagine a more difficult line to toe than maintaining a dark sky tourist destination, and it's a metaphor for the challenge that's faced by every Michigan town with a view over one of its magical lakes. You invite the visitors to experience what makes your town so special, and then you cross your fingers and hope they don't crush it; a parade of a hundred headlights obscuring everything the drivers of the cars came to see.

We wake up the next morning to pedal south for the first time in a while, and we are still north of the places where the people are. The water off to the left is the Grand Traverse Bay, a calm and reaching finger of Lake Michigan. It is the same water, and yet, it is somehow different. Quieter, perhaps. A deep layered blue crawls off toward the horizon, teal froth at the sandy shallows and dark navy farther out, where the depths begin.

There is no traffic on this road and there are fewer homes, the land filled instead with ungridded trees, clusters of birches, their white bark peeling papery strips that dangle and twitch in the breeze. Pines tower behind those, their needles catching and filtering the rays of sunshine that have tried to break through the clouds. The air smells like wet stones.

The roadside is not dotted with mailboxes and there are not the rollaway trash bins waiting to be returned to a cluttered garage. Instead, it's an explosion of yellow coneflowers, purple asters, and sprays of Queen Anne's lace. It cannot last like this forever, and it doesn't. As we continue south, we see a few more cars, a few more homes, and a few more beer cans on the road.

And then we're in Suttons Bay, a lake town so perfect it might be plucked from a film set. If it was snowing, I would be sure I was in a Hallmark Holiday movie, and I would watch very carefully to make sure I didn't get my wife stolen by some hunky pine tree farmer dressed exclusively in plaid shirts ready to teach her the true meaning of the Christmas.

Suttons Bay is so pristine that it almost feels unreal. The streets are lined with tidy storefronts painted in soft, cheerful colors – mint green, robin's egg blue, and butter yellow. Hanging flower baskets swing from old-fashioned lampposts, their blooms impossibly bright, as though someone has cranked the saturation entirely too high.

Every shop window is curated with care: handmade pottery, local wines, artisanal soaps. Smiling women parade one after another out of the bookstore and none of them have purchased a book. A couple strolls by, laughing softly, their golden retriever trotting beside them as if scripted into the scene. Even the bay, its shoreline a crescent of white sand and smooth stones, sparkles in the sunlight as if it is only there to read its lines.

The smell of chocolate and lavender and sugar and coffee is intoxicating, a siren's song after 600 miles of cycling. I want to love Suttons Bay from the moment I see it, but not as much as Suttons Bay wants my love. There's something too flawless about the town, too insistent. The perfection creates a strange distance, like the place has been dressed up for a visitor it wants to impress. The town feels curated even more than it feels built.

Not that there's anything wrong with any of this. People love Disney World, after all, and Suttons Bay is just as magical at a fraction of the cost. But then, people don't actually *live* at Disney World. Do they live here?

Increasingly, the answer to that last question is no. The demand for short-term rentals has driven Suttons Bay's home prices into the Michigan stratosphere, and even as more dwellings are built year-over-year, the town's permanent population has started to drop. Many of the people who work in the shops cannot afford to live in the town, and many of the people who own the rental homes are doing so from a great distance.

Efforts have been made to curtail the short-term rental industry, but results have been mixed. It's easy enough to push back against an effort that wants to turn your neighborhood into the world's largest hotel, right up until the moment the town decides *you* can't sell your home for enough money to retire early and send your kids to college.

This problem is not terribly unique to Suttons Bay, and versions of the issue are found throughout Michigan's perfect lake towns. They are becoming places increasingly owned by outsiders and operated for outsiders.

We learned all this from a man working in a nearby cheese cave, and the cheese was delicious. His story sounded a lot like the story a lot of people in Suttons Bay could have told. He was grateful for the tourists. His business wouldn't survive without them. And at the same time, his lease was just cancelled because his landlord realized he could make four times as much money listing the property on Airbnb. The cheese man was going to have to move out of town and commute in just like everyone else does.

None of this is the fault of the tourists, of course. They were invited here, beckoned by the iconic voice of Tim Allen sharing the undeniable allure of Pure Michigan. They come to escape the troubles of the world, not to consider their own tacit role in the socioeconomic terraforming that the tourism industry has wrought on the place that invited them.

The things that have made Michiganders rich have always come at a cost, from the lumber kings who toppled the forests to the factories that built fortunes while poisoning rivers. Left unchecked, tourism will bring wreckage of its own, a cost not hidden in soil or water, but in the hollowing out of places like Suttons Bay.

We pedal away from the town, the same way hundreds of thousands of other tourists will during the year, and if Suttons Bay has a problem, it won't be ours to solve. Anyway, I've got problems of my own to worry about. There are twenty miles left in today's bike ride, and I think I ate too much cheese.

CHAPTER SIXTEEN

TRAVERSE CITY

By the time we arrive in Traverse City, the place is a party, and the party has started without us. It's been like this for weeks now, and it will stay this way pretty much until the last of the leaves falls off the trees. There are about 15,000 people who live in Traverse, and many of them will spend their summer entertaining more than seven million visitors. In five months, more people will visit the Greater Grand Traverse region than live in Hong Kong. If Suttons Bay is a tourist town, then Traverse City is the metropolitan version of the same thing.

A few days after we leave Traverse, the National Cherry Festival will begin, and the town will bubble to a foamy simmer until it explodes. People from everywhere will come to sample cherry pie, cherry beer, cherry soda, cherry salsa, cherry cheesecake, cherry bread, cherry wine, cherry soup, pickled cherries, cherry ice cream, cherry sausage, cherry coffee, cherry mustard, cherry risotto, cherry butter, and of course, fresh picked cherries with stems to be plucked and pits ready to be spat just as far as possible.

A half million people will eat and drink and enjoy shows on a main stage that has featured international superstars like Sheryl Crow, Pat Benatar, Foreigner, REO Speedwagon, Stone Temple Pilots, Flo Rida, Nelly, and Chicago. They'll watch fireworks over the bay and retreat each evening to hotel rooms and campgrounds and short-term rentals that cast a net across a radius of dozens of miles. The festival will leave no doubt that Traverse City is the Cherry Capital of the World. When the visitors fly into Traverse – and many of them do – they will arrive at the Cherry Capital Airport.

It's a far cry from Traverse City's wild roots, a lumberjack outpost founded in 1847, once considered so remote that for a decade, it was only accessible via boat. Traverse had a post office before it had a road, and they planted cherry trees before they had either. It was a good enough life for a few decades, at least until the old growth trees were gone, and the lumber barons had moved west. By 1880, Traverse City was well-connected to the state's road system, but the problem was that no one really needed to go there anymore.

So many of Michigan's lake towns have a story like this one. They were built by wood, then decimated along with the forests that birthed them. In the wake of the destruction of Michigan's bounty of natural resources, some towns were rescued for a time by manufacturing concerns. Others became agricultural hamlets. Still others remained in decline for decades until the tourists discovered them all over again. But each of them had to survive somehow and someway in the decades between the time when the forests were cleared and the tourists arrived.

$*$ $*$ $*$

Perry Hannah was born in Erie, Pennsylvania in 1824; but by 1851, he was operating the sawmill at Traverse City and was well on his way toward becoming one of Michigan's premier lumber barons. His company would clear more than 50,000 acres of pristine forest by the time there was nothing left. For his part, Hannah would make a lot of money.

Early Traverse City was a company town, and besides controlling the businesses that processed the wood, Hannah also owned the general stores and the banks. It was a recipe ripe for cruelty and exploitation, but it would appear that Perry Hannah did not seize the opportunity to mistreat his workers. Anyone who was bold enough to make the trip to Traverse City would be given a job and paid fairly.

It's tempting to tell simple histories of complicated places, to consign entire eras of development and destruction to single decisions made by individual stakeholders. It's rarely that simple. History ties itself in complicated knots with dozens of competing personalities warring with forces political, religious, social, cultural, scientific, and economic.

But in this case, it might really be that simple. Perry Hannah originated Traverse City's first industry. He built its downtown himself, and plenty of the buildings that he put up are still there. He was Traverse City's first Village President. He was its first Mayor. He was the first man to represent Grand Traverse County in Michigan's House of Representatives.

Hannah Park and Hannah Avenue are named in his honor, and a sculpted statue of the baron stands watch over a downtown intersection. The plaque honors him as the Father of Traverse City, and the plaque does not exaggerate.

Perry Hannah never abandoned his child. When other lumber barons skedaddled for virgin forest in the west, Hannah remained in Traverse City. He never went anywhere else. He died in Traverse in 1904, and he is buried in the city's Oakwood Cemetery.

He never stopped fighting for the city either. By 1885, Hannah recognized – like everyone else in his line of work – that Michigan's so-called inexhaustible natural resources were nearing their end. Traverse had been built around the timber trade and its solitary lumber baron as much as any one place could be. They were nothing if they didn't have the trees, and Hannah knew better than any of his hired hands that they were about to run out of trees. Something else was going to have to save the town, and there was only one man with the power to do it.

Perry Hannah went to the statehouse in Lansing, pulled every political string he had, and called in every favor he was ever owed. Hannah's influence proved to be enough, and by the end of 1885, the Northern Michigan Asylum was established just beyond the reaches of Traverse City's downtown.

The facility was a boon for a town that needed one, and in those early years, the population of the Asylum even outstripped the population of Traverse City. The Asylum also brought reliable government funding and plenty of good jobs. The 400,000 square foot facility needed plenty of hands to keep it running and the hundreds of patients needed plenty more.

During the next hundred years, Michigan experienced plenty of growth and so did the population of patients deemed to be mentally unstable. The Northern Michigan Asylum grew along with that population, eventually encompassing 1,100 acres and 1.4 million square feet of floor space.

Of course, the Asylum also saw its fair share of tragedies, stemming from a fundamental misunderstanding of mental health. Doctors performed the fullest menu of harrowing and unproven treatments, including unconsenting lobotomies and electroshock therapies. But given that these so-called therapies were going to happen somewhere, it was a good thing for Traverse City's economy that they happened where they did. The Asylum held 3,000 patients at a time and employed hundreds of locals during the in-between years – the time after the lumber barons went out of business but before the tourism boom brought Weird Al to town to play the Cherry Festival.

The psychiatric facility finally closed in 1989, having served more than 50,000 patients in barely more than a century. The buildings are still standing and are remarkably well preserved. They've been redeveloped as a hip mixed-use neighborhood featuring apartments, senior living facilities, commercial space, a local goods shopping center, and restaurants that sell things like cherry-avocado toast and local wine. During the busiest parts of the tourist season, the former Asylum is crowded to capacity. There's a joke in there somewhere, and that joke is not lost on the locals.

Also not lost on the locals is the fact that the Asylum – and everything the Asylum has become – is directly attributable to Perry Hannah. Between the Asylum and the downtown, if you have a meal at a local restaurant in Traverse City, there's a good chance you're in a Hannah building. If you buy a novelty T-shirt or a coffee table book or a bottle of olive oil, that probably came out of a Hannah building too. If you attend a church downtown, it's very likely one he helped finance. And should you have the misfortune to die in Traverse City, your body could well end up in Hannah Perry's former home, now in use as a funeral parlor at the corner of Sixth and Pine.

*   *   *

Tourism is not at all a new phenomenon in Michigan. People have been running away from busy cities to beautiful sunny beaches for centuries. The tourists have been coming here for a while, but it's only in the last 40 years that their behavior has begun to change.

It used to be that lake life meant something like a true escape. Mom, dad, a couple kids, maybe the family dog; all loaded

155

up into a station wagon, laden with everything they'd need for a week away. If there was a stop in town, it was to pick up milk and to fill up with gas before the trip back home again. Other than that, you played on the beach, read your books, and worked your puzzles on the dining room table.

It was unconscionable to consider leaving the hustle and bustle of the city to head for a place like downtown Traverse City, filled with stores and shops and crowded sidewalks. After all, the wall of people was what you'd come to avoid, and no one went on vacation for the privilege of waiting in a queue *somewhere else.*

But by the 1980s, tourist attitudes changed. Suburbanites from quiet subdivisions found novelty in the kinds of quaint downtowns that they didn't think still existed. They came *for* the towns. They discovered favorite restaurants that they would visit year after year after year. They told their friends. They saw the water less, but they saw the city more.

Sociologists could write entire books about how this societal shift started to happen, but what's most important to me is *when* it started to happen. By the middle of the 1980s, just as the Asylum was preparing to close, the tourists started to alight upon Traverse City in numbers its shopkeepers had never seen before. All they had to do now was to seize on the moment, and that's exactly what they've done ever since, planning elaborate festivals, investing in new restaurants and breweries, and shrewdly establishing themselves as the epicenter of tourism operations in a region that spans several counties. They built gorgeous bike paths that invite people like me to jump from one perfect destination to another over the course of a long weekend. Traverse City was rescued again, just in the nick of time, and this time they rescued themselves. Perry Hannah would be a proud father if he could see it.

156

As for their relationship with the tourists, Traverse City seems to have struck a balance that plenty of other lake towns have struggled to find. I'm told by one restauranteur that unlike in smaller towns, Traverse City's size allows most of its establishments to remain open year-round, even if that comes with reduced staffing.

"It goes a long way toward keeping the goodwill of the locals when they know that a place is willing to stay open even when the out-of-towners stop coming for the winter," he says. "And besides, Traverse City has been filled with crazy people since the 1880s. I guess you could say we've gotten used to it."

CHAPTER SEVENTEEN

THE MORMON PIRATE KING OF BEAVER ISLAND

The morning brings with it a chill as the sun starts to stretch over the bay. We leave Traverse City to the sound of men pounding tent stakes, but those sounds are soon a rhythm of the past, swept up as always by the whir of tires on pavement. The road is smooth and easy, lined with oaks and pines. The bay opens to our left as we turn to the north, the road still and flat.

The cool of the morning lingers into the afternoon, a misty breeze off of the water, not pulling and not pushing, just whispering, a reminder that this is the north. The tourists still come, but they spend less time on the beach. Children still swim happily, but their parents are counting down the minutes until it's time to get out of the water. Sidewalks remain filled with people wearing shorts, but they're also wearing sweatshirts.

There are no clouds, neither overhead nor reflected in the waters, and the crisp morning has only served to turn up the saturation on another impossibly blue Michigan sky. On all sides, the blue above melts into the blue below, and the water is calm.

Our road is a geographic tightrope, straddling a narrow northern isthmus, buttressed on all sides by everything wet. To the west, the Traverse Bay will give way to Lake Michigan. To the east, Elk Lake and Elk River. It's a miracle that one hasn't swallowed the other, and before the cafes are even serving lunch, we're into the town of Elk Rapids, an entire community squeezed into the half mile between one sandy shore and another.

The town has everything a lake town is supposed to have— tidy houses lining picturesque streets, each thoroughfare pointing

159

toward a quaint downtown dotted with shops and cafes and places to buy, fix, or sell a boat. But somewhere in the middle of all of it, there's something else, something that feels like it doesn't belong.

That something else is the thing that was here first.

We stop our bikes and walk toward the remains of what was once a massive behemoth of a blast furnace, constructed in 1872, then among the largest such facilities in the state. The furnace is silent now, what's left of it anyway, and its gaping maw has been turned first into an accidental monument and then later into a deliberate one. Its bricks, weathered by decades of sun and snow, seem to hold whispers of the furnace's fiery past. Haphazard grasses creep around the furnace's base, reclaiming a place that once hummed with the fullest measure of Michigan's industrial ambition. All these years later, the chill air still carries the faint tang of iron.

The furnace had been part of the Elk Rapids Iron Company, one of the largest iron-producing operations in Michigan during its time. It took in local iron ore, limestone, and charcoal – burned with an almost insatiable hunger – and churned out pig iron, fueling a booming industry. The heat would have been oppressive, the noise relentless, as the town lived by the bellows' breath and the furnace's rhythm. A plaque near the furnace recalls a time when Elk Rapids pulsed with industrial energy, its residents moving to the cadence of production. Standing here on a cool, quiet Elk Rapids morning, it is impossible to imagine the smoke and fire that once engulfed this place, or the violent clanging sounds of the industry that drove it.

But those days are long gone. By the late 19th century, the iron industry shifted to larger operations downstate and to places with easier access to coal. The furnace fell silent, and Elk Rapids changed. The town moved on, turning toward the orchards and fields, embracing the slower rhythms of farming. In time, the tourists came, drawn by the glassy waters and the charm of a place that only *feels* untouched by time.

Those tourists seem to be just waking up as we pass through Elk Rapids, the crisp air enough to persuade them to have another cup of coffee before beginning on the important business of the leisure of the day. Beyond the town, the road curves gently, pulling us along the parts of Michigan where the trees are thicker and the homes fewer. The morning sun rises higher, but its warmth does not carry as far as its light.

Miles slip away and whole days would slip away if we'd let them, but then we see what we've been looking for, what we've been expecting to see on this day. There, on the side of the road, is a green sign, weathered, unimpressive. We stop anyway. We read the words, even though we already knew what they were going to say. We are crossing the 45th Parallel, halfway between the Equator and the North Pole.

Beyond the sign, the road bends, and so do our expectations. Beyond the 45th Parallel, I had imagined the promise of this division; untamed beauty and tranquil isolation. I had foreseen a place where the pines grew taller, their needles darker, their scent richer. I had imagined a place where the land whispered a wilder hymn, where the rivers froze harder, where the stars were closer and brighter and untamed.

Maybe that's what it used to be anyway, and maybe that's why so many people of means have erected such extravagant homes along northern Torch Lake. For my part, I can't say I blame them. Torch Lake might be the most perfect body of water I've ever seen, its shores clean, its water clear, its horizon pristine. Stand with your toes in the water and look down at your feet, and if you didn't feel the cold wet against your skin, your eyes wouldn't believe there was

161

water there at all. Torch Lake persuades you that you are the first person to discover it, even as you stand between a pair of massive houses, each with docks and tiny yachts.

Lake estates like castles sprawl along the water's edge, the tastes of their owners on full display. Each mansion seems to compete with the next, all glass and grandeur, and if you're impressed with the excess of the architecture that faces the road, just wait until you see what they've built to look out at the lake.

Docks stretch arrogantly into the water, hosting boats larger than some of the cottages we passed on the way. The stillness of the lake is mirrored by the stillness of the estates, eerily immaculate, as if life itself is kept at bay.

It is a strange kind of beauty, this stretch of Torch Lake. The water still glimmers like a jewel, its surface catching the sun and scattering it back in shards of turquoise and sapphire. But it feels trapped, hemmed in by artifice and excess, as though the lake itself were caught in the grip of those who own its edges.

I am not alone in lamenting the way that people have tried to own the most perfect parts of Michigan, and yet, this is not new. People have tried to own the most perfect parts of Michigan since the Europeans got here. They cut it down, hunted it to extinction, extracted it, and left it for dead.

At least this time, they found something they loved and decided to protect it. As easy as it is for a pair of vagabond cyclists to jealously judge the wealthy with a lakeview, the truth is that those same people have kept Torch Lake clean and healthy and gorgeous for decades and have diligently developed systems and strategies to keep it that way for decades to come. If it wasn't lake houses, it would be a Nestle bottling facility charging Michiganders four dollars at a time to drink their own water.

None of that is to forgive the some of the most blatant architectural sins along the waterfront, but in the long history of America's desecration of natural resources, there are a lot worse things than turrets on a lake house.

*   *   *

We've been cycling through Antrim County since we got to Elk Rapids, one of those unfortunate counties given a new name to erase an original moniker than honored a tribal chief. Antrim County took its name from Antrim County in Ireland, named in deference to the increasing numbers of Irish immigrants coming to Michigan in 1843. It was a hasty name change, and lawmakers didn't even bother to spell the name of the county correctly in the original legislative act. For eight years, Antrim County was, legally, "Antim County".

But before that, it was Meegisee County, named after the Ojibwe chief whose signature appeared on the 1821 Treaty of Chicago and the 1826 Treaty of Mississinewas. Meegisee's name was stripped from the county that used to be his home shortly after his tribe was relocated. The renaming was a strategy to attract settlers, fearful that pioneers would be wary of choosing a place with a difficult to pronounce and obviously tribal name. It seems that Meegisee was not American enough for the Americans, and that's a shame. His name is literally translated, "bald eagle."

*   *   *

The road tightens and squeezes as we approach Charlevoix, another place where all roads converge into one, another quarter-

163

mile strip between two lakes, and this time there's only one bridge – and a drawbridge at that – to move drivers from one side of the Round Lake Channel to the other. Travelers inch toward the town, some of them pointed toward destinations in Charlevoix, others just passing through, destined for lake towns even further into The North. The whole ordeal is exactly the kind of automotive logjam that perfect vacations are supposed to avoid. The people in their cars are frustrated, and I'd like to imagine that they were even a little envious at the way our bikes flaunted the traffic. We pivoted onto the sidewalk and pushed through in a few minutes what would take the drivers half an hour.

And then we're there, standing on a sidewalk, breathing in the magic of Charlevoix, a town whose name rolls off of your tongue like an incantation. Excepting the long line of steaming minivans that bisect the city center, everything in Charlevoix is everything its name seems to suggest – enchanting, elegant, cosmopolitan, sophisticated.

Linguists could write dissertations on this place, and I am not one of them, but I assure you that none of modern Charlevoix would exist in the way that it does today if the place had kept its original name: Pine River.

The Charlevoix name summons feelings of enchantment, and those feelings come to life in Earl Young's Mushroom Houses, the architectural antithesis of the turreted lake houses we saw just a little while ago. Young constructed the homes during the first half of the 1900s, each one a whimsical blend of stone, wood, and luscious curved lines. Each one is an expression of the earth, a fairytale cottage that might be home to an elf or a gnome. In one way, it's easy to look upon a Mushroom House and believe that it doesn't belong. A Mushroom House is just so much different than

164

what you'd expect a house to be. But in another way, the Mushroom House challenges you. Maybe it's all those other houses that don't belong, gawdy and ostentatious representations that obscure God's perfect earth.

The Charlevoix name also summons sophisticate vibes, and these run right through to the region's core. The nation's elite have been vacationing here since the 1880s, beginning with the Chicago Club and later the Belvedere Club. The wealth of the visitors delivered wealth unto the town, an opera house, a golf course, a bathhouse designed by Frank Lloyd Wright. It's hard to believe that these accoutrements would have ever visited themselves on a place called Pine River.

During Prohibition, Charlevoix became one of the preferred destinations for Chicago gangsters who needed to lay low for a while. They'd set up for days and weeks at a time at The Colonial Club, and they'd be welcomed so long as they were willing to kiss the ring of the man who owned the place.

John Koch, the club's owner, might have hosted men who wanted to keep a low profile, but that didn't mean he was one of them. His personal car had the license plate number "2", second only to Michigan's governor, and he would have taken "1" if he could get it. Besides the gambling and the scheming that happened at his club, Koch also operated a converted lumber barge that functioned as a floating speakeasy during the years that alcohol was outlawed throughout the nation. Again, it's hard to imagine a man as showy as this every setting up shop at a place called Pine River.

Charlevoix's name change is an undoubted branding success story, one that could be studied in marketing classes in universities. It's a town with a great name that's manifested all of the associations that its name conjures. But let's not get too far ahead of ourselves

165

celebrating the advertising geniuses who came up with the decision to rename their northern village. After all, they never intended to build this type of town when they relabeled the place.

They just wanted to distance themselves from the unfortunate association with religious violence.

*   *   *

In the mid-19th century, long before the fine resorts and the mushroom houses and while Elk Rapids was still smelting iron, the town of Pine River was still wild and untamed, a pioneer outpost covered with dense forest and softly rolling dunes. Pine River was the domain of hardened men, willing to do the work, to endure the winters, to survive the elements.

But if that wasn't a tough enough way to live a life, there was another even more grueling option. Beaver Island sits just 23 miles off of Charlevoix's shoreline, 55 square miles of the most ruggedly beautiful and ruggedly rugged landscapes that Michigan has to offer. It's a remote place even now, and it was even more remote then. That made it the perfect place for the coronation of James Jesse Strang, the self-proclaimed Mormon pirate king of Beaver Island.

James Strang began his life far from the Great Lakes, born in New York in 1813. A lawyer by trade and a dreamer by nature, Strang was drawn to the burgeoning Church of Jesus Christ of Latter-day Saints. After the assassination of Joseph Smith in 1844, Strang declared himself the man's rightful successor, citing a dubious letter from Smith naming him as the new prophet. While most of the Saints followed Brigham Young westward to Utah, Strang led a splinter group northward to the shores of Lake Michigan, eventually settling on Beaver Island.

At first, Strang and his followers sought peace and isolation. Beaver Island, with its thick forests and sheltered harbors, was an ideal refuge. Strang crowned himself king in 1850, donning a crimson robe and a tin crown in a theatrical coronation. He ruled his kingdom with a mixture of charisma and iron discipline, implementing strict laws and claiming divine authority for his actions. His Kingdom flourished and grew powerful enough that Strang was even able to force tithe payments from the gentiles who were not a part of his community.

To his followers, Strang was a prophet. To his enemies, he was a despot and a threat.

Strang's kingdom quickly attracted attention, and not all of it was welcome. The Mormon settlers clashed with local fishermen and traders over resources and trade routes. Strang's practice of "consecrating" property – essentially confiscating it for his church – earned him enemies among non-Mormons, who began referring to his followers as pirates. Whether Strang himself engaged in piracy remains a matter of debate, but stories of his followers raiding nearby settlements and plundering ships spread like wildfire. According to one legend, Strang's followers would sink ships, then rescue female passengers and force them into marriage.

The newspaper reported that all of these rumors were false, but of course, Strang ran the newspaper too.

In the middle of all of this, Strang was pulling legal strings at Michigan's statehouse, calling upon his legal knowledge to legitimize his community. He successfully moved the county seat to Beaver Island and oversaw two elections that elected him to the Michigan House of Representatives in 1853 and 1855. Amazingly, both votes were unanimous.

To the Strangites, their King was only growing in authority and influence. To the rest of Michigan, it was a bad joke. Strang's four years at the statehouse began four years after he became a publicly avowed polygamist and three years after he proclaimed himself the "King of Heaven and Earth."

By the early 1850s, tensions between Strang's kingdom and the surrounding communities had reached a boiling point. For a short time, Strang even helped to ease tensions between Native Americans and mainland Michiganders, each willing to put their conflict aside for the cause of hating this new man who was calling himself a king.

The town of Pine River became a focal point of the conflict between Strang's people and Everyone Else. Situated at the mouth of a strategic waterway connecting Lake Michigan to the inland lakes, Pine River was a vital hub for trade and travel. Strang's ambitions threatened to choke off this lifeline, and the settlers of Pine River decided they could endure his rule no longer.

The final straw came in the summer of 1853. A group of Strang's followers, emboldened by their leader's rhetoric, seized a shipment of goods bound for Pine River. The settlers, incensed and desperate, banded together to form a militia. They would not wait for the distant authorities in Detroit to act. They would take matters into their own hands.

The Battle of Pine River, as it would come to be known, was less a battle and more a chaotic skirmish. Armed with hunting rifles, axes, and a smattering of old muskets, the Pine River militia set out to confront Strang's men. They launched their attack at dawn, rowing across the narrow channel to a small camp of Strangites on the mainland. The fighting was fierce but brief, a whirlwind of smoke, shouts, and the acrid smell of gunpowder. When the smoke

168

cleared, the Mormon camp lay in ruins, and the settlers of Pine River declared victory.

The cost, however, was high. Several lives were lost on both sides, and the violence shocked the region. The settlers of Pine River, once proud of their stand, soon found themselves haunted by the bloodshed. They wanted to distance themselves from the memory of that day and from the man whose name had become synonymous with conflict. They'd never be able to attract people to a town whose name was only famous for ugly conflict.

The town rechristened itself Charlevoix, after the French Jesuit explorer Pierre François Xavier de Charlevoix. The new name was meant to evoke civility and exploration, a clean break from Pine River's immediate tumultuous past. It seems like it worked.

As for James Strang, his reign did not last much longer. In 1856, he was assassinated by two disgruntled former followers, shot in the back on a dock on Beaver Island. His death marked the end of his kingdom. The remaining Strangites were forcibly evicted from Beaver Island by an angry mob, their homes burned, their dreams scattered to the winds.

Nearly two centuries later, the Strangite movement is dwindling, but it's not evaporated. Six congregations remain – now headquartered in Wisconsin – and more than 100 followers continue to proclaim the angelic ordination of James Strang.

But Beaver Island was so much more than just the Kingdom of Strang. It was home to generations of Irish immigrants who found it in themselves to leave Europe so long as they could find another cold, rocky, rainy island to live on. It wasn't hard to begin a life on Beaver Island as long as you could endure the conditions. All you needed was a fishing pole and a little patience. Once upon a time, Beaver Island was the largest supplier of freshwater fish in the

United States. Generations of fishermen lived and thrived on Beaver Island before, during, and after Strang.

Their way of life survived the Mormon pirate King.

It wouldn't survive the lamprey eel.

By the mid-20th century, the waters surrounding Beaver Island had long since ceased to echo with the gunfire of skirmishes or the hymns of Strang's kingdom. Instead, they reverberated with the cries of fishermen watching their nets come up empty. The culprit was a creature that seemed almost mythical in its destruction – the invasive sea lamprey. First spotted in the Great Lakes in the early 20th century, the lamprey eel invaded the delicate ecosystem like a marauding army, and by the 1940s and 1950s, its impact had become catastrophic.

For generations, the fishermen of Beaver Island had thrived in the bountiful waters of Lake Michigan. The island's fishing industry was its lifeblood, with whitefish and lake trout forming the backbone of both local sustenance and trade. Families passed down the craft of fishing like a sacred inheritance, their lives tied to the rhythms of the lake. But the lamprey eel changed everything.

Lampreys are parasitic fish, long and eel-like, with circular mouths lined with rows of teeth that latch onto larger fish. Once attached, they drain their host's blood and bodily fluids, often killing the fish in the process. In an ecosystem unaccustomed to such a predator, the lamprey had no natural checks. Populations of lake trout – apex predators crucial to maintaining the balance of the Great Lakes – plummeted. Entire schools of fish vanished, leaving Beaver Island's fishermen with little to catch.

The devastation wasn't immediate, but it was relentless. Throughout the 1940s, fishermen noticed their hauls growing smaller. By the 1950s, it became clear that the lamprey eel was not

170

just a nuisance but an existential threat. Nets that once teemed with fish now emerged slimy and empty. Families that had relied on fishing for generations found themselves facing ruin. The island's economy, already fragile, began to collapse under the weight of this ecological disaster.

Efforts to combat the lamprey were slow to take effect. Scientists and conservationists eventually developed lampricides, chemical treatments that targeted lamprey spawning grounds without harming native fish. These measures, along with physical barriers and trapping, gradually reduced lamprey populations. But for Beaver Island, the damage had already been done.

The residents began leaving in droves around the 1940s. You already know who took their place and you know it was the tourists.

CHAPTER EIGHTEEN
HEMINGWAY'S MICHIGAN

When Ernest Hemingway sat down at his typewriter to tap out the words that would become <u>A Moveable Feast</u> – his final love letter to the Paris of the 1920s – he did so to capture the magic of a time and a place that could never be repeated. He ate clams in bohemian cafes, washed down with a liter of white wine. He alighted upon Gertrude Stein at her home. He met a drunken and erratic F. Scott Fitzgerald. His marriage crumbled in the City of Love.

Given the way the canon of western literature developed throughout the 20th century, Hemingway's Paris was a kind of literary Eden, the birth of everything that would come next. Ernest Hemingway was in the very epicenter of all of it.

It was 1957 when the author began his work on <u>A Moveable Feast</u>. He started writing in Cuba, took his draft manuscript with him to Idaho and later Spain. It took three years to get the draft completed, and all the while, Hemingway was remembering and reliving – often painfully – his time in Paris while looking out the window upon some of the most beautiful and scenic places in the world. His mind may have been in a Paris of the past, and his body might have been in Spain and Cuba and Idaho, but his heart was always somewhere else entirely.

His heart was always in Michigan.

Sometimes it took a long way to get there, but for Ernest Hemingway, eventually, all roads led back to Michigan. The first chapter of <u>A Moveable Feast</u> begins with the man sitting in a Parisian café, drinking rum St. James, and writing about Michigan. <u>True at First Light</u> is set in Africa but recalls the taste of sweet Michigan apple cider. In <u>Islands in the Stream</u>, when the lead character is asked when he had been the happiest, he remembers his days on Lake Michigan as a boy. No matter where Hemingway went – and he went to an awful lot of places – it was always Michigan that bubbled to the top of his imagination.

Michigan made Hemingway. It taught him the power of the clean lines and the tough simplicity that defined his revolutionary writing style. You can trace it all back to the Michigan lakeshores and forests where young Hemingway spent his summers hunting, fishing, and absorbing the unspoken language of the outdoors. His characters, like his prose, are shaped by that landscape: rugged, stoic, and always aware of what lies beneath the surface. If Paris gave him his sophistication, Michigan gave him his spine. It's not much of a stretch to say that Hemingway's style – spare, direct, and true – feels, at its core, *Pure Michigan.*

Hemingway's Michigan begins in Petoskey, and our bike ride could have only ever had one destination once we arrived. We push through the town, our tires tossing arcs of water behind us, a light pattering of rain drumming softly on our helmets, and then there he is, standing proudly in Pennsylvania Park.

The statue presents a young fellow, not so recognizable compared to the man he would become. The statue is modeled after a 1920 photograph of a 21-year-old Ernest Hemingway preparing to leave Petoskey for a job in Toronto. It's the purest version of Hemingway that the town can call its own, frozen in bronze, tall and confident, duffel bag in hand. The rain trickles down his forehead and pools in the creases of his jacket. In the truest expression of Hemingway's masculine Stoicism, he is unbothered by the wet.

It's been a hundred years since Hemingway vacationed here as a boy, since he returned to the town to recoup from the injuries he suffered in the Great War. But Petoskey is still Hemingway's town. Cuba and Paris and Key West have continued without him, built new histories, erected statues and monuments besides his. Even the bullfights went on in the wake of the man's death. But in Petoskey, it's like he never left and like he never had to grow up.

Of course, before Hemingway arrived, Petoskey was a town unto itself, shaped by the rhythms of the land and water. Long before it became a summer retreat for Midwestern families like the Hemingways, this place was home to the Odawa people, who named it *Petosegay*. The word is said to mean that Petoskey is the place "where the light shines through the clouds," except on this day, it doesn't. The grey of the sky has fallen into the grey of the lake and the horizon has been lost to sea.

Petoskey's growth as a town accelerated with the arrival of the railroad in 1873. When George Gage, a reporter for the *Grand Rapids Times* made the trip to tell of the opening of the rail line, he was awestruck by Petoskey's beauty. He described the way the glistening snow loaded the tree branches as a scene from *Tales of Arabian Nights* and declared Petoskey to be the home of the Million Dollar Sunset. Adjusting for inflation, that makes a modern Petoskey sunset worth more than $26 billion.

Almost overnight, the small settlement transformed into a bustling summer destination for industrialists, writers, and anyone looking to trade city grime for fresh lake air. The grand *Perry Hotel*, still standing today, was built in 1899 to accommodate the influx of tourists. It boasted modern luxuries including hot water, electricity, and postcard views of the bay. Hemingway himself would have seen the hotel towering over the town square, a symbol of Petoskey's golden age. He even paid 75 cents for a room at the Perry in 1916 before joining his family at the lake.

But this was more than just a resort town. It was a land of rough and tumble lumberjacks and fishermen and hunters, the kinds of hard men with macho bravado that Hemingway would write into characters throughout his career. And that bravado sometimes came with a cost. Massive deforestation wrecked Petoskey the same way it wrecked everywhere else.

For the passenger pigeon it was even worse. Lumber barons had wiped out their most fruitful nesting grounds, and the gunmen came to shoot them down while they looked for a new place to live. In 1878, Petoskey witnessed one of the last great nestings of passenger pigeons near Crooked Lake. During this event, hunters killed an estimated 50,000 birds daily over several months, leading to a total slaughter of approximately 7.5 million pigeons.

The scale of the slaughter was staggering. One hunter was reputed to have personally killed a million birds, earning $60,000, a fortune at the time, and equivalent to over $1 million today.

It was 1905 by the time Hemingway would form lasting memories from his trips to the family's cottage at Walloon Lake and their daytrips into the big town of Petoskey. Hemingway's Michigan was a wild place, at least to hear his stories tell it, but it was tamer than it had once been. The thick forests were thinned and gone. There were no longer the flocks of birds that could blot the sky.

But for a kid from Oak Park, Illinois; it might have been the most magically wild place in the world. That's the Michigan you find in Hemingway's *Nick Adams* stories, full of streams that twist through shadowy forests, lakes that shimmer under wide-open skies, and woods alive with the soft sounds of unseen creatures. It's a landscape that looms larger than life, both in his memory and in his fiction, where every trout feels like a trophy and every day holds the promise of adventure.

But Hemingway's Michigan wasn't just a backdrop; it was a forge. It shaped the way he saw the world and the way he wrote about it. In those summers on the lake, he learned the rhythms of the natural world, the hard edges of survival, and the quiet power of solitude. Michigan made Hemingway, and then, it seems that for the rest of his life, whenever he picked up a pen, Hemingway tried to remake Michigan.

This Michigan was a place of endless summers – long days spent fishing the swift-running streams, hunting in the woods, and swimming in the cold, clear lakes. At Walloon Lake, in the family's cottage affectionately called *Windemere*, young Ernest found the freedom to roam, to test himself against nature, and to soak up the kinds of details that would later fill his fiction: the tug of a trout on a line, the crunch of boots on pine needles, the way the light hits the water at dusk.

Petoskey became the boy's town, a hub where his family would resupply or take in a show at the theater, a place that hummed with the energy of summer tourists but still felt small enough to belong to him. It was here, years later, that Hemingway returned after his time as a Red Cross ambulance driver in World War I, carrying physical and emotional scars from the front. In 1919, Hemingway came to northern Michigan to heal, to write, and perhaps to figure out who he was now that the war had changed him. He rented a room at the boarding house of Mrs. Eva Potter in Petoskey, just a short walk from the lake, and spent that winter honing his craft.

This was the Hemingway who still believed in beginnings, who spent his days writing stories by hand and his nights socializing with the locals or courting the daughter of a wealthy Petoskey family. Her name was Hadley Richardson, a woman he would soon marry and take with him to Paris. Their marriage certificate is on display at the Charlevoix Historical Society Museum.

For all of Hemingway's adventures – the bullfights in Spain, the safaris in Africa, the cafés of Paris – there's a strong argument that his years in Michigan were the best of his life. Those summers on Walloon Lake and his days in and around Petoskey were free of the complications that would follow him: no literary rivalries, no failed marriages, no battles with fame or his own unraveling mind. In Michigan, life was simpler. It was fishing at dawn, a crackling campfire at dusk, and water so clear it seemed to cleanse the soul.

When Hemingway wrote about Michigan later in life, there was a tenderness in his prose that's hard to find elsewhere. The *Nick Adams* stories, often rooted in his own memories, reveal a longing for that boyhood world of trout streams, pine woods, and quiet companionship.

The years that followed were brilliant but also brutal. Hemingway would go on to reshape modern literature, win Pulitzer and Nobel Prizes, and become a larger-than-life figure. But he would also stumble through broken relationships, alcoholism, and the relentless pressures of his own legend. When it all grew too heavy, his memories of Michigan remained a kind of refuge. In a way, Hemingway spent the rest of his life trying to recreate what he had in those early years: a sense of purpose, of innocence, of being close to something real.

For Hemingway, northern Michigan wasn't just a place; it was a time – a fleeting, golden moment when the world made sense. It's why Petoskey's Hemingway statue is my favorite of all of the monuments that have been built to the man. It's not hard to imagine him there with you, young and unbroken, with the whole world in front of him and Michigan at his back.

There are two required pilgrimages that come with any trip to Petoskey, and we've already seen the statue. That means it's time to head to the beach, even in the rain. We're not the only ones walking through the sand with our heads down, and as an outsider, I'm not really sure that I'd be able to recognize what I'm looking for if I found it.

To my untrained eye, Petoskey stones look like any other rock: gray and unremarkable when dry. But wet them in the lake's cold water, and the fossilized corals reveal themselves – tiny, intricate flowers frozen in time.

Petoskey stones are fossils – coral from a long-gone sea that covered Michigan over 350 million years ago during the Devonian period. Back then, what is now northern Michigan sat near the equator, submerged beneath warm, tropical waters teeming with life. The coral that became Petoskey stones, *Hexagonaria percarinata*, thrived in these shallow seas, forming massive reefs that stretched across the prehistoric landscape.

When the seas receded and the earth shifted, these coral colonies were buried under layers of sediment, where they slowly fossilized over millions of years. The hexagonal patterns we see today are the remains of the coral's skeleton, each tiny "flower" marking where a single coral polyp once lived – feeding, growing, and building its limestone home.

It took glaciers to bring them to us. During the Ice Age, massive glaciers scraped across the land, grinding rock, soil, and fossils along with them. As those glaciers retreated, they scattered Petoskey stones across Michigan, polishing them smooth and leaving them to rest along the shores of the Little Traverse Bay. Today, every stone you pick up on the beach is a fragment of an ancient world, shaped by time, water, and ice into something inescapably beautiful.

Anyway, we didn't find any.

But as we walked back up from the beach, dripping and empty-handed, we discovered something even better: the McLean and Eakin Bookstore, one of those wholly local, warm shops where time seems to slow down the moment you step inside. The smell of paper and wood greeted us, and rows of shelves crowded with well-loved spines stretched toward the corners.

Of course, they had Hemingway. A whole shelf of him – *For Whom the Bell Tolls, The Nick Adams Stories, The Old Man and the Sea* – his words stacked up like artifacts of another era, waiting to be picked up and rediscovered. And as the rain continued to trickle outside, I didn't need much to be convinced. I opened *Nick Adams* and asked Hemingway to deliver some wisdom for the rainy day. He delivered. He always does:

"It was not raining inside the café."

Indeed it was not.

CHAPTER NINETEEN
TUNNEL OF TREES

We wake up in a Petoskey that has earned its Odawa name. Shining rays of golden sunshine stream through rapidly breaking clouds, brightening the earth and for the first time in a few days, warming our spirits. By the time we're finished with breakfast, the clouds will be a faded memory. The wind, too, has shifted, now blowing steadily toward the north. On this day, Michigan has conspired to deliver a perfect bike ride. I smile at my perfect companion and I don't even need a second cup of coffee to persuade me to hit the road. There has never been a more inviting day, and I don't know it quite yet, but there has never been a more inviting route either.

The wind is carrying us and we are sailing. Michigan trees rise up, full and green. It's a brief summer in northern Michigan, but when it comes, it's stunning. The air is heavy with the sharp, clean smells of pine, soft bark, and dew drops on cedar leaves. It's a forest in full voice, every scent carried on the northbound wind.

The land north of Petoskey is well protected. To the west, Petoskey State Park stands between us and Lake Michigan. To the east, a parade of nature preserves, one bleeding into another and then another. This part of the state is only going to grow more beautiful with time, a promise that's difficult even to imagine.

Tall, thick trees wave and rustle in the breeze, the leaves shimmering like a thousand green coins in the sunlight. The air is alive with the soft hum of insects. Light filters through the branches, spilling gold onto the road ahead like something sacred. We round a bend and discover a deer standing still in the center of the road. Her coat is the color of late summer fields, and her ears twitch as she watches us. We coast toward her, neither pressing the pedals nor pulling our brakes. She is not afraid of us, and she is barely curious. If it wasn't for the oncoming car, she might have let us path within an arm's length. But there is that car, and so she turns, steps softly back into the trees, then disappears as if she was never there.

Bike rides like this one usually have a moment that pulls you out of the dream. You round a bend or crest a hill, and you stumble onto a slum tucked into the trees, a smoke-belching factory, a reeking manure field, or a sprawling suburb choking on traffic and strip malls. It's the cost of beauty, the reminder that the world isn't all green and gold. But on this ride, the moment never comes. There's no break in the spell. No ugly interruption.

There's really just the one town between now and the end of the day: Harbor Springs, Michigan. It's a small village tucked into Little Traverse Bay, the lake shimmering at its edge. We stop at a lakeside café for cappuccinos, and we are not the only ones with such an inclination. Men shake hands and smile; couples find each other at a bustling lunch counter. An entire bachelorette party orders copious quantities of black coffee, either preparing for a very long day or recovering from a very long night. People are gathering here, the same way they always have, ever since the Odawa people called the land L'Abre Croche – literally, "The Crooked Tree".

The Crooked Tree stood as a landmark, a guide for the Odawa people traveling these shores. Its bent shape was a signal, a gathering place, and a marker of home. This land, rich with forests and streams, offered everything they needed: timber for their canoes, game from the woods, fish from the bay, and fertile soil for their crops. If the people who administrate the nature preserves that buttress Harbor Springs in all directions have their way, this land will become those things all over again.

Maybe it's already beginning to happen. There's a farmer's market that's taken over a downtown street, vendors dressed in flannel with attractive displays of the bounty of the earth. Just outside of Harbor Springs, proud trees reach to kiss the clouds, not fearful of the lumberman's axe and saw. Dark, rich, peaty soil is beginning to replace the thirsty, sandy stuff that only recently marked the forest floor. Wild turkeys boast proudly at the side of the road, unafraid of the traffic. Deer move silently through the underbrush. A black bear sighting is rare, but not impossible. Foxes dart across clearings, hawks circle overhead. Streams teem with fish and the occasional pair of playful otters.

It's almost enough to feel like a kind of complete restoration, but there's something missing, something gone even further away, and something that's even more difficult to imagine ever returning.

The original people are gone.

The ones who found that Crooked Tree and built lives and societies around it were driven out, and their villages were dismantled as soon as they left. Sometimes it happened before they were even gone.

Andrew Blackbird, the son of an Odawa chief, wrote about this loss in his book, *History of the Ottawa and Chippewa Indians of Michigan*. He described how his people, through treaties they often didn't fully understand, were forced to cede their land, uprooted from the shores that had sustained them for centuries. In his words:

"We were deceived, out-generaled, and deprived of our homes, and at last compelled to leave our beautiful country and beautiful home as a prey to the white people."

We ride past Blackbird's house, now a museum, on the way out of town. It's a small piece, a tiny anchor that connects Harbor Springs to an irreplaceable part of its past. And then, propelled by caffeine and tailwind, we're back into the wilderness, forests broken by vineyards broken by beachfront and returned to forest once again; all of it impossibly living and lush

Northwest of Harbor Springs, the trees are thriving and they seem to squeeze the road, their canopy overhead enough to shade the midday sunlight almost entirely. We are into Michigan's famed Tunnel of Trees.

You've seen this road plenty of times in your life, featured in dozens of commercials for the newest American sportscar. The Ford Mustang Mach-E stalks this road on your television, its electric engine quieter than the hum of its tires or the chirp of the birds overhead. The car traces each sweeping curve of the narrow unstriped road, pockets of glittering sunshine sneaking through the trees and sparkling off of the vehicle's flawless paint.

A professional driver guides the thing up a steep ramp and around another bend, emerging now into the briefest of openings, the infinite sapphire lake visible for a fleeting, dreamy moment; and then gone again as the car swoops back around another gentle bend and disappears into a long gauntlet of soaring sentinel trees.

The commercial only lasts 30 seconds, but if you manage to make it this far north, you can experience all of it, unceasing and uninterrupted for 15 miles. Ashley sips from her water bottle, and then, with the knowing smirk of the driver in the car commercial, she charges up the road. We are ready to pretend to be race cars.

We cruise through the thickest part of the canopy, where only pin pricks of light peek through the above, a hundred tiny beams of sunlight screaming like tiny missiles for the ground. We push hard on the pedals. We do not pull the brakes. The lake is never far away, but it disappears for minutes at a time, only to reappear at a sudden outcropping, breathtaking, arresting.

It goes on like this for a full hour.

I want to come back in the fall, ride it again when the leaves turn from green to yellow to orange to red. I want to come back in the winter, when the air is crisp and smells of pine, when limbs hang limply, weighted with fresh and untouched snow. I want to be here in the spring, when life buds in pink and white and yellow, to feel the first rush of spring warmth against my skin, to experience the sudden chill of the total shade and the euphoria of the brief and unexpected sunbathed openings in the canopy that melt everything all over again. I want to ride back to the beginning and experience it all in reverse and then I want to ride back to the end to catch everything that I missed the first time. Someday I will.

But not this day. We've got pressing plans to look at a very long bridge, and we've still got some number of miles to go. The wind will push us as far north as it possibly can before the day is ended. The rest of the ride continues along quiet, forested roads. We detour down a gravel path a few miles out of the way to get past a failed bridge. We see: coyote, deer, rabbits, turkeys, cardinals, field mice, a bald eagle, a few mailboxes, very few houses, almost no cars.

I've ridden my bike in a lot of places, through Denver's Red Rocks, alongside mountain streams in the thin air of Estes Park, across North Carolina's Blue Ridge Parkway and to the top of Mount Mitchell where the purple-grey horizon stretches even beyond infinity. I've dropped in among the rocky outcroppings of Ohio's Cuyahoga Valley, ridden to very top of the highest mountain in Vermont, and pedaled a bicycle close enough to wet myself with the mist of Niagara Falls.

But this was the greatest bike ride of my life.

CHAPTER TWENTY
MACKINAC

Mackinaw City smells like deep-fried fish and confectioner's sugar. On the sidewalks there are too many bodies pressed too closely to one another. Children with chocolate-stained fingers shove pieces of fudge into their mouths even before they've finished chewing the morsel that was already in there. Parents shout into cell phones about everything they were supposed to leave behind on vacation while gaggles of confused tourists navigate intersections as if they've only just discovered crosswalks. There are bells ringing and people chattering, and in the distance, ferry horns. In one storefront and then another you can watch them pull saltwater taffy in mesmerizing loops through windows smeared with children's face prints. A toddler cries over spilled ice cream that now belongs to the bees, and a teenage boy argues with his mom because she won't let him buy ninja stars, which are apparently a thing you can purchase here. This is Mackinaw City and Mackinaw City is a lot of things, but by the end of the day, it's mostly just sticky.

Long before this part of Michigan was overrun by tourists in bucket hats and children covered in melted fudge, it was a place of profound significance to the Anishinaabe people. The Straits of Mackinac – the narrow passage connecting Lake Michigan to Lake Huron – wasn't just a pretty spot for sunset selfies. These were sacred waters, a vital artery for trade, travel, and survival. The Anishinaabe, including the Odawa, Ojibwe, and Potawatomi peoples, saw this place as the beating heart of their world. They didn't just stumble upon it; they thrived here for centuries, living lives of complexity, tradition, and ingenuity. Spoiler alert: none of those traditions involved saltwater taffy or ninja stars.

Even the name of the place has been whitewashed. The native people called all of this Michilimackinac, an ancient word that literally means "Big Turtle", and precisely the same big turtle whose back we've been cruising for the better part of two weeks. When that word was deemed too much of a mouthful for the Europeans, they first shortened it to Mackinac, and when that name proved too difficult to spell, they gave it a more phonetic spelling: Mackinaw.

That helps to explain why, today, you can travel to Mackinaw City, and from there you can visit Mackinac Island or Fort Michilimackinac. If you ever hear anyone pronounce any of those places with a hard 'C' at the end of the word, feel free to tell them they're doing it wrong. With so much of Michigan's native history wiped away, the least we can do is take the beautiful words they left for their places and pronounce them correctly.

The Europeans arrived here in the 1600s, and during the coming centuries, French and British colonizers transformed the sacred ground into a hub for the fur trade. Indigenous people were integral to this new economy, but make no mistake, they weren't exactly benefiting from the arrangement. Their partnerships with European traders walked a tightrope between exploitation and extermination with a side of smallpox.

For the next several hundred years, the history of the region would receive one coat of white paint after another, a parade of propagandist storytelling that lionized French voyageurs, valiant British soldiers, and pioneering Americans. In recent years, there have been efforts to tell Indigenous stories, but it's difficult to recover a history that, in many cases, has been deliberately buried.

The French outpost at Fort Michilimackinac has been reconstructed as a tourist attraction where actors in tricorner hats wax sentimental about the days of colonial rule amid the romantic blastings of old-timey muskets. The history tries to be honest, tries to tell that this is a place that was taken from the native people, but it somehow obscures the story about the time in 1763 when the native people took it back.

By the 1760s, the British had displaced the French as the dominant European power in Michigan. The Brits took colonial arrogance to a level that the French could have only dreamed about, and the English alienated the indigenous people almost immediately.

Unlike the French, who had built relationships through trade and diplomacy (albeit self-serving ones), the British treated the local people as an afterthought. They restricted trade of essential goods like gunpowder and ammunition and generally acted as though they were entitled to the land without offering anything in return. Unsurprisingly, resentment festered.

When Pontiac launched his war to try to drive the British out, the Anishinaabe people of northern Michigan were persuaded to join his cause, quickly launching an incredible and improbable attack against Fort Michilimackinac. They used baggatiway, a traditional lacrosse-like game, as their Trojan Horse. The game wasn't just a sport; it was deeply rooted in their culture and was often played during gatherings and ceremonies. To the British soldiers stationed at the fort, the contest looked like a harmless spectacle, a friendly match to celebrate a festive occasion. The Anishinaabe even invited the soldiers to watch, lulling them into a false sense of security.

On June 2, 1763, the game unfolded just outside the fort. The players and the spectators moved closer and closer to the gates as the match grew more intense. At one point, the ball "accidentally" flew over the fort's palisade wall. This wasn't unusual; games were often spirited and chaotic. A few players ran to retrieve it, and the British guards, unbothered, allowed them inside.

But these weren't just athletes. They were warriors, armed with weapons concealed beneath their garments. Now that they were inside the fort, the battle was on. Within moments, the Anishinaabe overwhelmed the guards and opened the gates, allowing more warriors to pour in. The British garrison, caught completely off guard, was no match for the organized assault. By the end of the day, the Anishinaabe had taken the fort and reclaimed control of the area. They held the fort for more than a year before the British were able to take it back.

Later on, the churlish Brits established a new, more protected fort on Mackinac Island, and after the War of 1812, that fort and the island were firmly and finally in the hands of the Americans. The Anishinaabe, once exploited by the French and mistreated by the British were at last removed altogether by their newest colonizers. The Mackinaw region remained a major driver of the fur trade until all of that dried up in the 1850s.

In the aftermath of the downfall of the fur trade, Mackinaw became equal parts fishing village and lumber town. Its borders became filled with rugged men, sawdust, mud, and a lot of swearing. In short, it wasn't quite ready to become the tourist town it was destined to be. It would take the arrival of the railroad before that could happen.

When the Michigan Central Railroad extended its tracks to Mackinaw City in 1881, it opened a door to the rest of the world. Goods, fish, lumber, and people could move in and out of the region with ease. Suddenly, Mackinaw was no longer just a remote outpost; it was connected. The railroad planted the first seeds of tourism. Wealthy city-dwellers, lured by tales of the region's natural beauty and healthy air, began arriving to fish, hunt, and escape the grime of industrial cities. They were the vanguard of what would become Mackinaw's tourist empire.

Meanwhile, Mackinac Island was stealing the show. The Grand Hotel opened in 1887, attracting the well-to-do with its wraparound porch, horse-drawn carriages, and promise of genteel leisure. Mackinaw City, in comparison, was the scrappy younger sibling, important, but not nearly as glamorous. While the island was hosting soirées, Mackinaw was still loading fish onto freight cars and figuring out what it wanted to be when it grew up.

By the time 1900 rolled around, Mackinaw City was a town in transition. It had industries, connections, and a budding reputation for natural beauty, but it hadn't fully embraced its destiny as a tourist haven. That would come later, with highways, motorcars, and the building of a certain iconic bridge. For now, Mackinaw was still rough around the edges, a place where fish guts and sawdust outnumbered souvenir shops, and where the future was just starting to take shape.

By the mid-20th century, Mackinaw City had shaken off its sawdust and fish guts and was ready to embrace its destiny. Enter the Mackinac Bridge. Completed in 1957, the bridge is a five-mile-long triumph of engineering, stubbornness, and a dash of insanity.

Before the bridge, the only way across was by ferry, and while ferries have their charm, they're not exactly efficient. By the 1950s, the ferry system was overwhelmed, and locals were tired of waiting for hours to reach northern Michigan.

Construction on the bridge began in 1954 and over the next three years, workers braved gale-force winds, bitter cold, and the occasional bout of seasickness to create what was, at the time, the longest suspension bridge in the world. The towers rise an impressive 552 feet above the water, and the cables would stretch more than 42,000 miles if laid end to end. Driving across it today, you're greeted by breathtaking views of Lake Michigan and Lake Huron, as well as the unsettling hum of tires on an open-grid roadway. It's not for the faint of heart. Our bikes aren't allowed on the bridge. We will only admire it from a distance.

I remember the first time I ever saw the Mackinac Bridge. It was a dinner cruise on a guided tour of the Straits of Mackinac, and I seem to remember that the food was not good. The woman with the microphone shared a lot of facts about the bridge, and then opened the floor for questions. An adorable eight-year-old girl with pigtails and bows raised her hand. The woman handed the girl the microphone so she could ask her question:

"How many people have committed suicide by jumping off of the Mackinac Bridge?"

The woman refused to answer the question and asked the DJ to turn on the music. The music was the radio, and the radio was tuned to the local Christian radio station. The answer the girl was looking for was twelve.

The bridge officially opened on November 1, 1957, and with it, Michigan's Upper and Lower Peninsulas were finally connected. This wasn't just a practical solution; it was a cultural revolution. Suddenly, the U.P. wasn't some far-flung wilderness. It was just a road trip away. Tourism boomed, and Mackinaw City, positioned at the foot of the bridge, became the gateway to adventure. From there, the tourist machine took over.

Not everyone on the modern streets of Mackinaw City is bound for the Upper Peninsula. Some will cross the bridge only to turn right around and drive back, eager to cross the feat off of their bucket list. Some won't cross the bridge at all. Many won't make the trip to the island. At some point in time, Mackinaw City stopped being the layover and started being the destination. It's been sticky ever since.

There are things worth seeing here – the bridge, the Island, the lighthouse, even the Fort – but somehow, the sideshow of the City has become the main attraction. The line for the Dairy Queen spills into the street even though there are at least twenty other local joints that sell ice cream. The places here make money, but I'm not sure how. I'll bet you could eat 4,000 calories in fudge samples moving from one shoppe to another without spending a dime.

We don't have time to play that game, as fun as it sounds. We're not staying in Mackinaw City. It was too difficult to find a room in town during this part of the season. We're onto another town and another story.

But before we go, we pause at a park just east of the bridge, just east of the invisible line that separates a pair of Great Lakes. The bridge is no doubt impressive, so long that you can't see to the other side, but I find myself looking beyond its deep columns and stretched cables. It's time to say goodbye to Lake Michigan, our steady companion for a week and then some.

Now we're onto the Huron. The Huron will take us home.

CHAPTER TWENTY-ONE
HURON

By the time we arrive at the restaurant in Cheboygan, there is a line of men in polo shirts already waiting to get in. They've come from either the boat or the golf course and possibly both, and there are kind of a lot of them. They already have reservations, they tell us, but they arrived 20 minutes before the place opened, just to be safe. This is at least a little alarming, mostly because we don't have reservations, and also because we don't have polo shirts either. It's my fault, and I should have known better. This isn't just *any* restaurant. It's the Hack-Ma-Tack Inn, and according to one list, it's the most iconic restaurant in the entire state of Michigan.

Originally constructed as a private hunting and fishing lodge all the way back in 1894, today's Hack-Ma-Tack has not strayed too far from its wild roots. It is exactly the kind of place that just feels like it belongs to a previous century, and it's also the kind of place that absolutely belongs on the Huron side of the state.

Stepping inside, it's as if the Hack-Ma-Tack has intentionally resisted the march of time. The air smells of wood smoke and pine. The warm, golden light from the chandeliers overhead makes everything feel a little cozier. The walls are paneled in dark wood, their surfaces adorned with relics of the past – faded photographs of trophy catches, mounted deer heads, antique cross-country skis that whisper stories of long winters and snowy adventure.

We're led to a table by the large picture windows, offering a view of the lush greenery and a crowded canal filled with boats captained by men with beers snuggled by drink koozies. The old hearth beside us exudes a comforting presence, weathered stones and iron tools telling of countless fires that have warmed this lodge

195

over the decades. It's easy to imagine weary hunters and anglers gathering here a century ago, returning from thick and faraway woods when they heard the clanging of the Hack-Ma-Tack's massive dinner bell.

Even the tables and chairs have character, their scuffed edges and creaky legs testament to the generations of guests who have passed through. Soon enough, the table will be filled with exactly the kinds of food you would expect – red meat, fresh fish, dark beer, smoky whiskey. This has long been an outpost for the rugged, and I don't know that I belong here, but I will certainly enjoy the food.

The hunters and fishermen who gathered in Cheboygan weren't the only rough and tumble souls to leave their mark on this part of Michigan. This was lumber country, after all, where towering white pines were felled and floated downriver by men who lived hard and worked harder. Pioneers carved out lives on this wild frontier, where every acre of farmland was earned through sweat and perseverance, and where every winter was a thing to be endured more than enjoyed.

Cheboygan and many of the towns along the Huron still call to those who crave a bit of that ruggedness for themselves. This isn't the Michigan of sandy beaches and umbrella drinks. Here, the draw is deep woods, winding rivers, and quiet lakes where a person can lose track of time and cell service all at once. It's a destination for those who don't mind roughing it or at least want to imagine they are. Even today, cabins and campsites outnumber resorts and hotels, and the appeal lies in the solitude of the natural world rather than the bustle of tourist hotspots. There are fewer places to purchase novelty T-shirts, and on the whole, it is less sticky. As far as I'm concerned, that's a very good thing.

But for all its rugged charm, Cheboygan also holds a few surprises, like how this little lumber town once built itself an opera house. Opened in 1877, the Cheboygan Opera House brought high culture to the northern wilderness, hosting everything from traveling theater troupes to symphonies. And if that wasn't enough, the town also boasts a Carnegie Library, one of the enduring legacies of the early 20th century philanthropic push to spread knowledge to even the most remote corners of America.

And then, of course, there's the ice bridge. In winter, when the Straits of Mackinac freeze over, Cheboygan becomes the starting point for one of Michigan's most daring traditions. The ice bridge to Bois Blanc Island is a lifeline for the hardy souls who call the island home year-round, and it's a test of nerve for anyone bold enough to venture across on snowmobiles or, occasionally, on foot. It's not an official road and there are no guarantees, just the sharp crack of the cold and the deep, quiet trust that the ice will hold. It's the kind of tradition that feels uniquely Cheboygan: part necessity, part adventure, and in some small part, shenanigans.

We ride out of Cheboygan pushing a headwind as we follow Lake Huron to the east and the south. On this side of the state, the spaces between the towns stretch further. We stop to limber our backs on the side of the road and meet a man who spent the pandemic making incredibly detailed, historically accurate scale models of local lighthouses, and then surrounding those models with figurines of beautiful, nude, Japanese gals. Why Japanese gals? Because those are the kinds of gals he likes to look at, and not those skinny ones, either, but real gals, busty, and with curves.
Those are his words verbatim, and that's what he decided to tell us – strangers he had never seen before who were only stopped next to his mailbox because they were experiencing back cramps.

Anyway, I found the guy's YouTube videos and can report to you that everything he described is exactly what he did and filmed and put on the internet. His work on the lighthouse model is well done and important and historically significant. I'm not so sure about the rest of it.

We ride quiet roads through stiff winds, disappearing only occasionally into wooded havens, then emerging onto sandswept paths that run almost right into the lake. The ride sparkles with colors and sounds and smells, and after weeks in the saddle, we are still not inured to it. The lake stretches before and beside us, 850 cubic miles of water, and we cannot see its end or its bottom. But remarkably, the lake will not be the thing that takes our breath away. 40 miles and not yet halfway into the ride, we stumble onto the biggest hole in the ground that I have ever seen, and I can't see to the end of this thing either.

Rogers City might not have the same name recognition as other spots along Lake Huron, but this small town packs a surprising punch. Known as the Nautical City, it sits at the heart of one of the most unique industries in Michigan. Home to the largest limestone quarry on Earth, the Carmeuse quarry sprawls across thousands of acres, a vast expanse of pale stone and heavy machinery that feels almost otherworldly. It's hard to overstate the scale of the operation. Trucks the size of houses crawl like ants along its terraced walls, hauling loads of stone that will eventually find their way into everything from roads to skyscrapers.

Each year, it produces more than 7 million tons of limestone, and since its founding in 1912, the site has yielded an estimated 800 million tons of stone. That's enough limestone to build the Great Pyramid of Giza 1,200 times over. The quarry's operations require its own fleet of freighters, which transport the stone to destinations across the Great Lakes and beyond, making it not just a local enterprise but a critical player in global construction and industry.

But Rogers City isn't just about limestone. It's a town with deep ties to the water, where shipping has been both a lifeline and a peril. The nearby waters of Lake Huron have seen their share of maritime tragedies, but few are as hauntingly present as the wreck of the Joseph S. Fay. This wooden steamer, built in 1871, was a workhorse of the Great Lakes, hauling iron ore through unpredictable waters

On October 19, 1905, the Fay encountered a powerful gale while navigating northern Lake Huron. Battling strong winds and towering waves, the vessel tried to seek refuge near Forty Mile Point Lighthouse, just north of Rogers City. It wasn't enough. The ship ran aground with such force that the wheelhouse and deck were torn from the hull and flung ashore. Miraculously, the captain and ten crew members were inside and survived the crash. Three others weren't as lucky.

By the time we stop for lunch at a quiet Rogers City beach, the wind has died down, and a quiet Lake Huron stretches calmly toward infinity. We breathe crisp, peaceful air into our lungs and we don't wonder about what's out there beneath the water.

For a small town, Rogers City has always managed to punch above its weight. Its Nautical Festival draws visitors every summer, a celebration of the community's maritime roots complete with parades, boat tours, and fireworks over the lake. And for history buffs, the Presque Isle County Historical Museum offers a deep dive into the area's German heritage, from the waves of immigration that shaped the town to the traditions that still linger today. But as has so often been the case, we can't stay, and so we climb aboard our bikes and keep going, just like the Lake does.

Just south of Rogers City lies Presque Isle, a peninsula whose name – French for "almost an island" – perfectly captures its geography and spirit. Presque Isle has long been a place of refuge and navigation, its shores first charted by French explorers who recognized its strategic importance on the Great Lakes.

Presque Isle feels like a place the world forgot. To get there, you have to go out of your way, down winding roads that hug the coastline and then dive into dense woods. There are no highways to hurry the journey, just the occasional deer darting across the road, and the growing sense that you're leaving something behind. The farther you go, the quieter it gets, until even the hum of distant traffic fades into the rustle of leaves and the calls of birds hidden high in the canopy.

It's that same sense of isolation that makes the lighthouses of Presque Isle so memorable. First, there's the Old Presque Isle Lighthouse, a modest stone tower built in 1840. Surrounded by dense trees and perched on the shore, it feels like something out of a storybook. Though it's no longer operational, its walls exude history, and the view from the top rewards those willing to climb its steep, narrow staircase. It's easy to imagine the keepers of long ago, tending the light through cold nights and thick fog, their only company the endless rhythm of the waves.

A few miles farther north stands the New Presque Isle Lighthouse, its striking white tower rising 113 feet into the air. Built in 1870, it's taller, brighter, and more imposing than its predecessor. It's also still active, its beacon cutting through the darkness to guide ships safely along the Huron shore. Walking the grounds, you can feel the weight of its history, the lives it saved, and the storms it weathered. The climb to the top offers breathtaking views of the lake, the forest, and the sheer remoteness of it all. Few people make the effort to get here, and that's exactly why it's worth it.

CHAPTER TWENTY-TWO
PAUL BUNYAN COUNTRY

On October 15, 1880, a beautiful evening at the tail end of one of Michigan's occasional Indian summers, the PS Alpena set out from Grand Haven on what should have been a routine voyage across Lake Michigan. Built in 1866, the sidewheel steamer was a proud symbol of the region's bustling maritime commerce, ferrying passengers, goods, and cargo between ports with efficiency and grace. But as she departed that evening, a sinister force brewed just beyond the horizon, a ferocious gale that would later be remembered as one of the Great Lakes' deadliest storms.

The storm, later dubbed "The Big Blow," raged across the waters with winds howling at near hurricane force. Waves towered over 30 feet, crashing down uncaringly and indiscriminately on any vessel unfortunate enough to be caught in its path. For the Alpena, there was no escape. Buffeted by the tempest, her wooden hull groaned under the strain as the waves smashed over her decks. By dawn on October 16, she had vanished beneath the roiling surface, taking with her an estimated 80 souls. It was one of the deadliest shipwrecks the Great Lakes had ever seen and became among its most notorious. More than a century later, the shipwreck has never been found.

A few days after the boat went down, chunks of its payload began to wash up on the sandy shores of Holland, Michigan – crates of apples, splintered lifeboats, an entire piano. The tragedy refused to be forgotten, new bits of the boat's cargo showing up on beaches for months and years after storms out over the water.

In 1909, nearly thirty years after the Alpena went down, its paddlebox nameboard washed ashore in the midst of the violent, crashing waves of the violent, crashing night before. The milelong stretch of shore has been known as Alpena Beach ever since.

The whole episode is a tragedy, no doubt, but it's proved a tremendous boon for Henry Schoolcraft and his made up Native American words. The word Alpena is one of his creations, one of those words that doesn't mean anything, but is supposed to sound like it does.

Besides the sunken ship and the Lake Michigan beachfront, there were at least two other boats named Alpena, there's a county named Alpena, and the town of Alpena is situated on Lake Huron just a dozen miles south of Presque Isle.

The lake towns on the Huron side of the state are as well-equipped as the ones on Michigan's sunset coast, but it seems like a lot fewer people know about them, and in some ways, that might make them even better. It was at Alpena that we had our best meal of the entire trip – at the Red Brick Tap & Barrel. This is a cool town, and maybe the only thing that could make it cooler is if it still had its original name. The town of Alpena used to be named after the water feature just off of its sandy shore. It used to be called Thunder Bay.

Thunder Bay: Two words that sent shudders through even the most hardened sailors. The waters off of the Alpena shoreline were treacherous and seductive. Each morning the locals would watch the glittering sunrise with bated breath, wondering aloud if this morning would bring another calamity. At least 200 times, it did.

Thunder Bay: Where the weather is fickle and violent, where winds whip and wail just miles from a quiet coast, and when the weather is clear, it is no less dangerous. Rocky reefs snag schooners and shifting sandbars ground vessels without rhyme or reason. It's shallow out there for a while and that's exactly the problem. The edges of Thunder Bay are far enough from the mainland to be subject to the whims of wild weather, but its depth or lack thereof means that storm-tossed ships can be driven against the unyielding shoals in an instant. Often, they are.

The town was still called Thunder Bay all the way back in 1861 when a boat called the Albion was lost to the sea just beyond the Huron horizon. The weather had been clear enough when the schooner set to its journey delivering a full cargo of pine logs to Detroit. The ship was barely away from the shore and not yet out of the bay when the squall appeared on the horizon, and the squall was coming fast. There would be no avoiding this one. The crew was doomed before the raindrops even began to fall.

The storm that overtook the Albion was relentless, a furious gale that ripped at her sails and drove her dangerously close to the shallow waters of the bay. Captain Spencer ordered the anchor dropped, hoping to ride out the storm, but the wind and waves proved too powerful. The Albion was dragged across a submerged reef and struck with a sickening crack. The hull splintered, and within minutes, the ship began to sink.

Accounts of the wreck suggest that the crew had little time to react. Clinging to debris, a handful of sailors managed to survive the night, eventually washing ashore in a state that wasn't quite dead yet. The rest of the bodies were never recovered, claimed by the icy waters of Lake Huron. The Albion's cargo of lumber – each buoyant log left to float upon the lake – scattered across the waves, some washing up days later on the beaches near Alpena.

The wreck marked the beginning of Thunder Bay's well-earned reputation as Lake Huron's "Shipwreck Alley". Just the mention of Thunder Bay was enough to conjure images of frozen, icy death; and for the people of the town of the same name, it was an association they were keen to distance themselves from. In 1871, they changed their name to Alpena. Nine years after that, when the PS Alpena became among the most infamous shipwrecks on the Great Lakes, the people of the town might have realized that, try as they might, they were never going to escape the echoes of nautical tragedy.

Today's Alpena has fully embraced its identity as a hub for some of the darkest moments of Michigan's maritime history, building a new industry around its storied past. At the heart of this effort is the Great Lakes Maritime Heritage Center, an impressive facility that serves as a gateway to the wonders of Thunder Bay. Part museum, part research hub, the center offers visitors an immersive journey into the history of the Great Lakes, showcasing artifacts recovered from the depths and interactive exhibits that bring shipwreck stories to life.

Guided tours aboard glass-bottom boats allow passengers to peer down into the clear waters of Lake Huron, where the ghostly remains of ships rest in silent testimony to the past. For the more adventurous, diving excursions provide an unparalleled opportunity to explore the underwater graveyard firsthand. The cold, fresh water of Thunder Bay has preserved many of these wrecks in astonishing detail, making it one of the world's premier destinations for shipwreck diving.

*   *   *

Hydrologically speaking, Lake Michigan and Lake Huron are really just one lake – one very, very large lake. And even though it's all the same water, we continue to discover subtle and delightful differences between the two lakes.

The Huron side is less populated, and for cyclists hoping to enjoy the view, that's good news. There are fewer neighborhoods and houses between us and the lake, fewer parks and fewer properties that might obscure the horizon. We ride south of Alpena, and when we cross back over the 45th Parallel, our slice of road is barely 50 feet from the water. It will be like this for most of the next 140 miles, and it will be perfect.

We skirt the shoreline of Thunder Bay then dive briefly inland to see Devil's Lake. Later, it will be Scarecrow Island, each waypoint named to remind you that this is the Huron, and the Huron is the domain of the rough and the rugged. The Huron is content to leave the finer beaches and fruitier cocktails to their statesmen on the other shore. The Huron is, and always has been, for a different crowd. After all, this is the home of Paul Bunyan.

Or at least it might be.

Now this is a more heated debate than you might think, and I've learned the hard way, receiving dozens of letters over the years from Paul Bunyan truthers, incensed by a piece I wrote about Bemidji, Minnesota in the year 2009. So when I saw the Paul Bunyan statue in Oscoda, I thought to myself…

"Here we go again."

Oscoda makes a pretty merited claim as the home of the legendary lumberman, providing actual evidence where other jurisdictions only offer claims. In 1906, James MacGillivray of the Oscoda Press, penned "The Round River Drive," a Paul Bunyan story that helped to establish the myth of the man in the public's consciousness. Only problem is, it wasn't the earliest mention of Paul Bunyan in the nation's newspapers. Two years before McGillivray biographized the giant, an uncredited editorial ran in the Duluth News Tribune about Bunyan strapping a pair of hams to his feet and skating around a milelong stove top to grease the cooking surface.

But the very earliest mention of Bunyan comes from Michigan, from Gladwin County, all the way back in 1893. The county might be some fifty miles from Oscoda, but that's nothing for Bunyan's lumbering strides, and the giant would have been more than happy to make the journey for the right trees.

Legend has it that during one particularly brutal Michigan winter, Bunyan discovered Babe the Blue Ox as a calf, frozen solid and stuck in a snowdrift. The poor animal was so cold that its fur turned blue. Bunyan thawed the calf out near a roaring fire, and the two were inseparable from that point forward, with Babe becoming not just his loyal companion but also a vital helper in his legendary logging feats. I can't vouch for the veracity of this story, but I can tell you that the part about Michigan winters checks out.

Like every town that claims Bunyan for its own, Oscoda boasts a long and proud lumber lineage, its logging legend entwined deeply with the Paul Bunyan mythos. During the late 19th and early 20th centuries, Oscoda was a bustling hub of the lumber industry, with massive log drives down the Au Sable River feeding the nation's insatiable appetite for timber. The Au Sable carves a long and meandering path through Northern Michigan's historic inland logging communities, almost as if Bunyan carved the waterway himself just to prove that he could.

It certainly wouldn't be the most outrageous of his exploits, a canon of stories that includes forming Minnesota's 10,000 lakes with his massive footfalls and carving the Grand Canyon by dragging his axe behind him on a particularly long journey.

Oscoda celebrates its claim to Bunyan's heritage with pride. Visitors can find statues and markers commemorating Bunyan's legacy, including a towering statue that greets travelers and keeps watch over the town. Oscoda's annual Paul Bunyan Days Festival further cements its identity, offering a weekend of events that pay homage to the lumbering heritage that shaped both the region and the legendary figure who represents it. If Oscoda isn't the birthplace of the lumberjack, it's at least the kind of place that might feel like home to him, and that's exactly the point. You come to the Huron for shipwrecks and chainsaw shows and to live a little like a lumberjack, or at least that's what we do.

At the pizza place in Tawas City, I'm confronted with a mountain of food that even Paul Bunyan might struggle to put away. If I'm remembering correctly, it was a baked potato wrapped in an entire pizza that stared back at me from my plate, but I suppose it's possible they concocted someway to wrap the potato around the pizza. I'm not sure, except that I remember it was a lot and that I did not finish.

CHAPTER TWENTY-THREE
THE THUMB

The old house stands apart, even on a long street filled with gorgeous and important homes. Brick walls soar high, as if equal with the trees, perched proud upon the stone wainscot that seems to rise from the earth. There is one turret and then another, a massive arched window, a brick chimney rising higher still. Stone columns surround wood columns surround the grand entrance to the grand home. The plaque in the front yard tells you what you already know – that this home is notable and historic and grand.

Modeled after the Romanesque design of the local Presbyterian Church, the home belonged to Fremont and Matilda Chesbrough, who moved in when construction was completed in 1891. It's a mishmash of a lot of different things, a maximalist design for a maximalist time. On the outside: heavy stones, warm orangey bricks, columns built from imported red marble. The confused roofline is broken first by the turrets and again by a pair of austere gables. And that's just the outside.

Inside: a wooden symphony in a hundred hues. White golden mahogany graces the front parlor, taking in and reflecting back the rich light that passes through the stained-glass window. The next parlor is dressed in cherry and walnut. Each banister, doorframe, cabinet, and ceiling a work of craftsmanship if not a work of art. In other rooms: leather walls, pink subway tile, curved turret benches.

From the top floors, look out upon the duchy from the turret windows and see another fine house and then another. Directly across the street is the Henry Clements home, a haughty Queen Anne. The houses posture and preen to assert themselves.

211

the same way their owners might have done in the heyday of their industries. You already know how Chesbrough and Clements made their money. They were lumbermen, and they had the homes to prove it.

Like so many places in Michigan, Bay City began as the domain of lumber barons like Henry Clements and Fremont Chesbrough. They came and saw and conquered and destroyed and built monuments to themselves and their success, then died just like the rest of us – Clements in 1901 and Chesbrough in 1934.

But as the lumber industry and its barons waned, Bay City would have to turn to another of its most precious natural resources to maintain relevance, one that would prove more permanent and more resistant to total destruction. The city's strategic position on the Saginaw River provided deep-water access to Lake Huron, and made it a natural home for shipbuilding. The same Saginaw River that once carried the logs to the mills now served as the lifeline for a thriving shipbuilding industry.

Bay City's early shipbuilding focused on wooden schooners – sleek, two- or three-masted vessels ideal for hauling goods across the Great Lakes. But as steel replaced wood as the material of choice, companies like the Davidson Shipbuilding Company and the Defoe Shipbuilding Company emerged as leaders in producing durable, high-tech ships.

During a pair of world wars, Bay City built vessels for the U.S. Navy, including destroyers, subchasers, and patrol craft. Defoe put the USS Skylark to sea in 1942, a new generation minesweeper for a new generation kind of conflict. In 1943, they launched the USS Hopping, believed by some to have been the fastest destroyer escort in the United States fleet at the time.

Besides their wartime production, Defoe made plenty of boats for personal and commercial use. In 1931, they constructed a 92-foot yacht for Montgomery Ward Chairman Sewell Avery. Avery called the boat the *Lenore*, but during the coming decades, it would become America's Presidential yacht. Eisenhower called it the *Barbara Anne*. Kennedy called it the *Honey Fitz*. Nixon called it *Tricia*.

Defoe built mammoth Great Lakes freighters into the 1950s and produced destroyers for the American and Australian Navies until the firm went out of business in 1972. One of its final boats – the HMAS Brisbane was in service until October 2021.

In the aftermath of World War II and the beginning of a new world order, the people of Bay City were proud of the way their hard work had helped secure the Allied victories that would sustain the American Century. That's probably why they got so upset when Madonna referred to the Bay City of 1958 as a "smelly little town."

You can't talk about Bay City without talking about Madonna, although there is a contingent of people in town who wish that wasn't the case. The Material Girl was born Madonna Louise Ciccone[5] in Bay City in 1958, and there's a sign announcing the fact along at least one road on the way into town. She wasn't in Bay City for long, moving first to Pontiac and then to Rochester Hills, a suburb of Detroit. The pop star has had a complicated relationship with Michigan ever since, and for its part, the state has had a complicated relationship with her.

Besides calling Bay City that "smelly little town", Madonna has at times called the Michiganders she grew up with "basic provincial-thinking people" and said that she missed "absolutely nothing" about growing up in Michigan. But at other times, she's insisted that she's been glad for her upbringing and has called

---

[5] Like many, I had always assumed that "Madonna" was a stage name. It isn't.

Detroit her hometown. Although she never lived inside the Motor City's limits, it is where she practiced ballet, had her first drink, and made many of her earliest forays into art and music.

Since her humble roots in Bay City, Madonna's lived quite a life – winning seven Grammys, a Golden Globe, making more than $800 million, and once kissing Britney Spears and Christina Aguilera in the same night on national television. Madonna's a big fish, to be sure, but plenty of Michiganders are willing to throw her back.[6]

Besides that roadside sign, Bay City has been reluctant to celebrate its most famous birth. Her disparaging remarks about the town aside, she wasn't here for long and never really made any attempt to reconnect. As for whether or not Detroit claims Madonna, it depends on who you ask. Some will be quick to point out that she's from the suburbs, not the city. Others will tell you that if Madonna doesn't want Michigan, then Michigan doesn't want Madonna. Maybe the greatest testament to Michigan's musical legacy is this:

They don't need her.

In January 2024, Madonna began to mend bridges with the place that raised her. During a one-night concert at Detroit's Little Caesar's Arena, Madonna waxed sentimental about the city and the state and credited her upbringing with teaching her to work hard, fight for herself, and live authentically. Toward the end of the show, in front of a sold-out crowd, Madonna breathed a sentence that was almost a plea:

"I hope you're proud of me, Detroit."

---

[6] It's also worth noting that many Detroiters are also quick to throw back Michael Jackson and his own complicated legacy, pointing out that he was born in Gary, Indiana. Remarkably, Detroit's musical legacy stands apart <u>even if</u> you don't count the Queen and King of Pop.

But of course, this isn't a chapter about Detroit. This is a chapter about Bay City, and at Bay City, we discovered the best ice cream of the entire trip. Michigan Cream & Sugar produces premium, small batch ice cream, sourced almost entirely from local ingredients, and the care they put into their product shows. Two scoops wrapped in a freshly griddled waffle cone while you sit on a bench and watch the boats dock on the river is a slice of heaven and not a small one. If Madonna hasn't made the trip back to Bay City to try this stuff yet, I'm not sure anything will persuade her.

*   *   *

Ashley and I say goodbye to Andrew and Erin and set off toward the east and the north. We're on our own the rest of the way, but the skies are clear, the temperatures are cool, and the forecast is promising. Even the wind will be on our side. In three days, we'll be back to Detroit, the place where all of this started, and we'll tell people we navigated the full circumference of that mythological turtle's back. All that's left to go is The Thumb.

The Thumb juts confidently into Lake Huron, forming The Mitten's namesake appendage, and the people here embrace their identity wholeheartedly. We pedal past signs advertising the Thumb Brewery, Thumb Industries, Thumb Cellular, and several branches of the Thumb National Bank. If you suffer a nasty fall on this part of the Huron and sever your opposable digit, then I've got good news for you. There's also the McLaren Thumb Regional Hospital.

There is not, so far as I can tell, a Thumb Bicycle Shop, and that has suddenly become a problem. After two weeks of cycling, hundreds of miles, and a shameful lack of bike maintenance; our mechanical luck has run out. Ashley's wheel is squealing and dry, not more than an hour after our tour has finally become a self-supported adventure. Bikes turned over, now on the side of the road, we attract gawkers who ask if we need help but have very little to offer. We tug and pry at the wheel, hoping to create enough of a gap to squeeze a few drops of chain lube into the wheel's bearings. Miraculously, the strategy works, but as we push off again, now some 90 minutes behind schedule, we have no idea how long our fix will hold.

If we run into any more issues, we're probably not going to be in a very good place to do something about it.

Bay City had been a good-sized town, one with all of the amenities we could have ever needed – bike shops, Ubers, even car rentals if it came to that. As we push east and north, we won't have access to any of those things again until we get to Detroit, and Detroit is three days away. We can only hope that the wheel will keep turning. Anyway, all is quiet on the road into Unionville, a small Michigan town named after a small Ohio city; a proud agricultural community for more than 150 years.

The town's agricultural lineage has roots that run all the way back to the ethnic Germans who'd been living in Russia's Volga River region since the years before the signing of the Declaration of Independence. Originally invited to Russia by Catherine the Great in the 1760s, the Volga Germans immigrated into Russia hoping to realize promises of land and religious freedoms. Those promises didn't last long.

By the middle of the 1800s, later rulers rescinded Catherine's kindnesses and snatched up the land that the Volga Germans supposed had been theirs. In exchange for the loss of their land, they received conscription notices. It was a raw deal. A century after relocating to Russia, many of the Volga Germans were moving to the other side of the world, and plenty of them would find new opportunity in Michigan's Thumb.

They would have a tough go of it. The Volga Germans spoke a unique dialect, a distinct blend of German and Russian that made it difficult to converse with other Germans in the New World. The language barrier forced a self-sufficiency on the Volga Germans who made Unionville their home and brought with them traditional dryland farming practices that could coax impressive yields with minimal irrigation. When those same methods were married to Michigan's famous abundance of water, the results were tremendous. Unionville became an agricultural star throughout the Thumb, and the Thumb became an agricultural leader throughout the state.

Their flagship crop?

The sugar beet.

Sugar beets don't look like much. Pull one out of the ground, and you'd be forgiven for thinking you were holding a misshapen, dirt-caked mutant radish. They're bulky, white, and knobby, and they're the kind of crop that seems more suited for livestock feed than for sweetening coffee. But inside that ugly root is gold, the edible kind. Packed with sucrose, sugar beets contain anywhere from 15 to 20 percent sugar by weight, making them one of the most efficient sources of refined sugar in the world.

While most people associate sugar with sugarcane – tall, swaying stalks growing in warm, tropical climates – beets thrive in cooler climates, making them perfect for Michigan's unpredictable seasons. And while sugarcane relies on vast plantations and backbreaking manual labor, sugar beets fit neatly into Midwestern farms, growing alongside corn and soybeans with the help of modern machinery.

It wasn't always this way. The sugar beet's journey from obscure vegetable to Michigan's cash crop started in 1747, when a German chemist, Andreas Marggraf, first isolated the sugar from the beets. It took decades for the discovery to turn into an industry, but by the early 1800s, Europeans were refining sugar from beets on a large scale. Napoleon Bonaparte, cut off from the Caribbean's sugarcane supply by British naval blockades, poured resources into beet sugar production, and the industry exploded. When the trend reached America in the late 19th century, Michigan was ready.

The state's first successful sugar beet factory opened in Essexville in 1898, just outside of Bay City. The industry spread fast. The soil in the Thumb was rich and fertile, perfect for the deep-growing roots of sugar beets. When we ate that indescribably good ice cream back in Bay City, it was delicious thanks to the magic of the sugar beet and the farmers who keep putting them in the ground.

Sebewaing, the next stop on our ride around the Thumb, is one of those towns that never let go of its beet-sugar roots. Home to a major processing plant and an annual celebration of all things sweet, Sebewaing throws the Michigan Sugar Festival every year in honor of the humble sugar beet. It's the kind of festival that embodies small-town Michigan – part agricultural fair, part block party, and entirely committed to having a good time. There's a midway with carnival rides, a parade with floats and marching bands, and, of course, a buffet of desserts that stretches an entire city block. At the heart of the festivities is the crowning of the Michigan Sugar Queen, a tradition that dates back decades and ensures that at least one person in town is contractually obligated to praise sugar beets for an entire year. Unfortunately for us and our bike ride through Sebewaing, the festival is over and the food is gone. But for the dentists, maybe their busy season is just beginning.

218

Sebewaing's ties to sugar beets go back to 1902 when the Michigan Sugar Company built a processing plant in town, one of many that cropped up across the Thumb in the early 20th century. The plant refined raw beets into pure sugar, employing generations of workers and making Sebewaing synonymous with the industry. Though smaller than some of Michigan's larger beet-processing hubs, Sebewaing maintained its reputation as a "sugar town," and even today, sugar beets remain one of the area's biggest crops.

We ride past beet fields for miles, and many of these are watched over diligently by the most majestic and impressive novelty statues in all of Michigan – a twenty-foot tall bantam chicken towers over a farmhouse, a family of stone white chickens stands gazing for an eternity over Lake Huron, a progressive clucker in rainbow gear celebrates a Pride Month that just ended. And then, at the end of a long line of inspired yard art, there's a psychotic paint-chipped Ronald McDonald wielding a chainsaw on the side of the road, grinning with a level enthusiasm that suggests he's either ready to carve ice sculptures or send us pedaling for our lives.

We don't stick around to find out.

For miles now, I've been tucked in closely behind Ashley's wheel, letting her break the headwind, resting in the draft. After two weeks in the saddle, my legs are running on empty. Somehow, squeaky wheel and all, she's still got plenty left in the tank. She leads us past the parade of chickens, away from the deranged fast food clown, and into Bay Port, home of the Fish Sandwich Festival. We're not here at the right time for this festival either, and that's probably for the best. Forty miles on a bike in rising heat is hard enough without a stomach full of fried fish sloshing around to make things interesting.

Beyond Bay Port, we're into Caseville, a place most famous for its annual Cheeseburger in Caseville Festival – a play on the Jimmy Buffett song. We're not here at the right time for that celebration either, and so we have to eat Fritos and Snickers bars from a gas station instead. We don't get to eat cheeseburgers twice a day for ten days, and we don't get to march in the Parade of Tropical Fools. The Cheeseburger Festival attracts tens of thousands of visitors every year, but this is just another Thursday in Caseville, and there are fewer than 700 people who live here. Still it's more civilization than we'll see for the next 25 miles, and that's about to become a problem.

Ashley's wheel has remained quiet, but my legs have been screaming. Mind over matter and only a few days to go, the view of the lake will sustain me, one leg and then the other, but why the hell are they so heavy? Mile after mile of gorgeous scenery, but I see none of it, my eyes trained only on the wheel in front of me. Stay as close as you can, but don't rub it. Stay as low as you can. Think aerodynamic thoughts.

We pass Sleeper State Park or at least that's what the map tells me because I can remember none of it. Just hold on. Just hold the wheel. Don't fall back. It gets so much harder if you fall back. Ease up the gears, pick up the cadence. Slow down the cadence, push a heavier gear. Do something. Do anything. Just keep moving.

So we do. We keep moving. We pedal along a perfect lake on a perfect day. We pass Port Crescent State Park.

And then, disaster.

CHAPTER TWENTY-FOUR
DISASTER

"Aaron, I'm getting a migraine."

"Shit. How long do we have?"

"Minutes. Ten. Maybe fifteen."

"Okay."

When Ashley gets a migraine, it comes on suddenly, but not without warning. It starts with an aura of light. After that, violent and twinkling stars start flashing in her periphery. The stars are a useful warning sign. It means everything is about to shut down. All we can do now is find a good place to let it happen. We are in the middle of nowhere, and my wife will be unconscious soon.

The map says we're a mile-and-a-half outside of Port Austin, and so we push to make it to town before the inevitable happens. We make it. We find a bench. Ashley collapses into it and swallows down handfuls of emergency meds that she carries with her at all times. The medicine will make her nauseous before it makes her sleepy. She does not cry. Her eyes are closed behind her sunglasses. The tiniest amount of light has become blinding. Her head is pounding, jackhammers beating against her skull from the inside. There is nothing I can do. I can only watch as she clutches her arms around her ears and waits to pass out.

And then the parade starts.

Not forty feet from our bench, the police motorcycles blare their sirens as if in competition with the firefighters wailing their emergency cries right behind them. A round of classic cars rev roaring engines, and a marching band plays a patriotic tune.

It's the Fourth of July in Port Austin, Michigan; and it's hard to imagine a worse time or place to land with a migraine.

A float hauls a Jimmy Buffett cover band down the parade route, and they play Margaritaville twice. The Delorean from *Back to the Future* is here for some reason, and it is loud as hell. Kids on trucks throw hard candy at us and spray Super Soakers intermittently. There is a cannon and the cannon goes boom. Our hotel is 30 miles away, and it's on the other side of this parade.

I am making phone calls, frantic and trying not to be. There is nowhere in this town to rent a car or get an Uber. There is nowhere to stay, not tonight anyway. Port Austin doesn't sell out very often, but it does on the Fourth of July. Finally I track down a tow truck driver who can give us a lift, but there's just one problem: His truck is hauling an entire Jimmy Buffett cover band through a parade, and he won't be able to get to us for several hours.

"That sounds about right."

"Sorry bud, any other day, I'd be right there."

"Do they play anything else besides Margaritaville?"

"They do not."

Seconds creep by like minutes and minutes like hours, and the torture I am feeling is nothing compared to Ashley's. I am helpless, and she is helpless. All I can do is stand in the way and absorb the blasts from the water guns.

*   *   *

Wherever we go, there are always Good Samaritans, and if not for the kindness of strangers, we would have never survived to begin this journey, let alone finish it.

In the aftermath of the parade, the gathered crowds disperse, and cleanup crews walk the route to sweep up the confetti and candy. That's when we met Jack, or at least when I met Jack.

222

Ashley can't remember meeting him. Jack had a camper van. Jack was on a trip with his wife. Jack was in the mood to give a ride to some strangers.

We were in the mood to let him, or at least I was. Ashley wasn't in the mood for much of anything.

*   *   *

We never did see Port Austin, didn't get to gaze upon its famous Turnip Rock. We didn't see Port Hope, either. We saw the inside of the camper van, and given the circumstances, the view was as wonderful as any vista we'd seen of the lake during the previous two weeks. Thirty miles in the camper van disappeared much quicker than they would have on a bicycle.

Just like that, we were in the town of Harbor Beach, standing in the parking lot at our motel. Our motel was unimpressive, and it was the best motel I had ever seen. Even a cramped shower goes a long way at the end of a day like that one. There's not a lot in the way of amenities in Harbor Beach, and whatever there might have been was closed on account of the holiday.

We wandered over to the Dollar General, tired legs taking measured steps, Ashley squinting through her sunglasses as we perused the aisles and chose TV dinners, Gatorades, bean dip, and ice cream sandwiches for dinner. We microwaved our meal and ate in our room with the lights off. Everything tasted like salt and mush, and the processed cheese burned the roof of my mouth. The air conditioner in the window was failing to keep the room cool. By 7:00 we were tucked into bed, somehow asleep two hours before the fireworks began, and if they boomed in the sky, they did not wake us. The next day arrived in the morning, just like it always does.

223

CHAPTER TWENTY-FIVE
MICHIGAN OLD FASHIONED

We're awake in Harbor Beach after a twelve-hour sleep, and our long nap has made all of the difference. Ashley's head is clear, my legs feel springy, and a clear sunrise greets a quiet town still recovering from the festivities of the night before. A breakfast of potatoes and eggs and coffee will take us through this day, just fine, thank you.

The Lake Huron coast has been our quiet companion for days, but by sunset, that will change, and we won't see a Great Lake again. Before today's ride is over, we'll leave behind the sleepy shoreline towns that have shaped the past few weeks, trading them for something bigger and busier – but not necessarily better. We won't finish this day in Detroit, but we won't be far from its shadow. It's hard to believe the circuit is almost over and harder still to believe that Detroit's sprawling metro is barely a day away. We're riding now through Forestville, and it's the smallest village in the entire state of Michigan.

As the name of the place suggests, Forestville was once filled with trees and was built by men with designs on cutting those trees down. It started with a sawmill and a post office, and it never really got much bigger than that. The village has a lakefront but no harbor, and so, once the trees were gone, there weren't a lot of natural advantages left. No deep-water port, no industry, no reinvention. Just a scattering of homes, a handful of quiet streets, and the stubborn remnants of a place that refuses to disappear. It's a miracle that Forestville survived at all, and it's a miracle all over again that the post office is still there.

This is still the romantic part of Michigan: shoreline roads, scenic overlooks, another shipwreck graveyard somewhere out there beyond the horizon. It was 1920 when the *Sport* – a steel tugboat nearing its fiftieth birthday – went down during a December storm. The crew escaped without harm, and for the most part, so did the boat, except for the 45 feet of water on top of it. A hundred years later, the *Sport* is still in pretty good shape, and it's plenty accessible to divers who are keen to survey the old ship and its artifacts, kept and preserved for prosperity. The *Sport* was the first shipwreck in Michigan to receive an official historical marker.

We continue our bike ride down the shore, still far enough away that we can't feel the rhythmic clanking and banging of the city, and we arrive in Port Sanilac, a very old town with a slightly newer name. This place used to be called Bark Shanty, named after the crude shelters that the original loggers used to call their homes in the 1840s and 1850s. And then, like they did in so many places, when the trees were gone, most of the men went with them.

But not all of them. Some of those men stayed, transforming their hovel into a town, then giving it a real name. Their shoddy bark homes gave way to log cabins. Thirty years after the entire population lived in homes made of stripped bark leaning against trees, Dr. Joseph Loop built a towering, elegant mansion filled with carved woodwork and Victorian grandeur. The mansion is still there, but remarkably, it's not the oldest remaining institution in Port Sanilac.

You wouldn't know it when you cruise through the downtown, pointed south toward a Detroit far beyond the horizon, but there's something special about the local hardware store. Raymond Hardware is Michigan's oldest, continuously operated since 1850, and still open today. The lumberjacks who lived in the bark shanties would have gotten their supplies from Raymond, and so too would the men who built the doctor's mansion. They came here when they built the town's Masonic Lodge and Town Hall in 1884 and again when the lanterns were lit at the Port Sanilac Lighthouse in 1886. Raymond was still there when the lighthouse was electrified in 1924. Its nails and screws are in the Port Sanilac Harbor of Refuge constructed in 1965. As Port Sanilac transitions into another of Michigan's picturesque tourist towns, Raymond is still there to help build its charming lake houses.

Raymond Hardware has a lot of things, but they do not have bearing grease for bicycle wheel hubs, and so we pedal on, hoping that whatever tenuous peace we have brokered with Ashley's squeaky wheel will hold for 100 more miles.

100 miles. That's how far it is to Detroit, the place where we started this loop, and the place where our journey will end. It feels further. None of the towns on the Huron is reminiscent of the churn of the Motor City. There are none of the whispers of Detroit's massive industries, no smokestacks on the horizon, no veins of freeway slicing through the virgin landscape. The Detroit of the previous century was a place built on factories and fortunes, and despite our proximity, there aren't a lot of whispers of those things as we roll into Lexington.

But that doesn't mean there aren't echoes.

This town was once the birthplace of one of the richest men in American history.

Charles Lathrop Pack wasn't a titan of industry in the way that Detroit's auto barons were. He didn't build factories or assembly lines, didn't mold steel into engines or drive men to toil on factory floors. His wealth came from something older, and you already know what it was – lumber.

227

Born in 1857, Pack inherited his father's timber empire, expanding it into a national juggernaut. At the height of his career, his holdings stretched across Michigan, Wisconsin, the Pacific Northwest, and even as far as South America. If there was money to be made in trees, Pack was making it. By the early 1900s, his fortune ranked among the largest in the country, making him one of the five wealthiest Americans before World War I. Pack's first act was impressive, but his second act would prove more important.

When the forests were depleted, Pack didn't just abandon them like so many others did. Instead, he pivoted toward conservation. He became one of the country's leading advocates for forestry management, reforestation, and sustainability at a time when those ideas were still considered revolutionary. His work helped lay the groundwork for modern environmental policy, long before conservation was a mainstream cause. It's all very honorable stuff, although the cynic in me has to point out that he didn't bother speaking about saving the forests until he'd finished making his fortune cutting them down.

During World War I, Pack launched the National War Garden Commission, encouraging Americans to grow their own food to support the war effort. The initiative took off, leading to the rise of Victory Gardens, which played a crucial role in feeding the country during both world wars. His passion for forestry led him to fund major conservation programs, promoting sustainable land use and responsible logging practices across the country.

Pack's time in Lexington was brief. He was born there, but didn't stick around for long, coming of age in Cleveland, and living and dying in New York. There are no monuments to his legacy in Lexington, and as far as Michigan goes, it's a state so filled with barons and billionaires that it doesn't really need this one to fill out the roster.

It begins to rain as we leave Lexington, drizzle chasing us as we skirt the last miles of a Great Lake that is about to run out. At Port Huron, we say goodbye to the waters that had become such a steady companion. The thirsty St. Clair River is drinking the lake away, and we'll follow its current the rest of the way. But first we've got to get through Port Huron, a city forged in fire, water, and a little madness.

Port Huron sits at the throat of the Great Lakes, where Lake Huron tumbles into the St. Clair River like an impatient giant shoving its way downstream. It's been a city of contradictions from the start – wild, stubborn, and just important enough to avoid being forgotten. Sure, Thomas Edison once lived here, but that's barely scratching the surface of what makes this place tick, and anyway, for his part, the inventor has said that he hated it here.

Long before any European ever set foot in the area, the Ojibwe people had this stretch of water figured out. They fished it, traveled it, and traded along its banks. Then came the French, who saw a business opportunity and wasted no time setting up a fur trade network. The British muscled in after the French and Indian War, and soon enough, Americans were pouring in post-1812, elbowing their way into the action. The St. Clair River has always been a highway for goods, people, and trouble.

After the War of 1812, the U.S. government, still jumpy about British influence, built Fort Gratiot to keep an eye on things. While it never saw any real battles, it did set the stage for one of Michigan's oldest and most vital pieces of infrastructure: the Fort Gratiot Lighthouse erected in 1829. Ships trying to nose their way into the St. Clair River needed a guiding light unless they wanted to end up decorating the bottom of Lake Huron. The Fort Gratiot lighthouse watched stoically as Port Huron grew into a maritime powerhouse. It remains the oldest lighthouse in Michigan.

For the next forty years, Port Huron continued to grow, providing the backdrop for Thomas Edison's adolescence from 1854 – 1864. He was an inventor even as a youth, although there were plenty around Port Huron who considered him a troublemaker instead. A young Edison once burned down a baggage car while experimenting with chemicals.

By 1870, the town's population had reached nearly 6,000 and the place had become an important hub on the Grand Trunk Railroad. Things were looking up for Port Huron, and then came the fires of October 8, 1871 – a bad day to be a wooden town.

Port Huron was one of many Michigan towns that burned to the ground that day, although it got it worse than many of them. A massive city-wide inferno leveled almost everything, but somehow the people of Port Huron found a silver lining in the tragedy. For them, the blaze was an architectural reset, and they set to rebuilding their city with better materials and bigger ambitions.

By 1891, they'd complete their most ambitious project to date, the St. Clair Tunnel, north America's first underwater rail tunnel. Built through sheer determination and a lot of men with pickaxes, it transformed the region into a critical freight link. Then in 1995, realizing that modern rail cars were too big for their 19th-century tunnel, Port Huron did what any practical city would do. It built another one, even bigger.

There's not just a tunnel here that points into Canada, there's also a gorgeous, audacious bridge. In 1938, the Blue Water Bridge linked Port Huron to Sarnia, Ontario, giving smugglers, tourists, and truckers a more efficient way to cross. As traffic skyrocketed, they added a second span in 1997. Today, it's one of the busiest border crossings in North America, a place where you can see a line of 18-wheelers stretching for miles while impatient drivers plot creative ways to cut in line.

The river beneath that bridge is no quiet backwater. It's a lifeline, a trade route, and at times, a lawless frontier. Escaped slaves travelling the Underground Railroad crossed these waters to Canada, leaving behind a country that considered them property. A century later, during Prohibition, the river became a freeway for smuggled booze, with bootleggers running whiskey across the border under the noses of federal agents. It's not hard to understand why. The river is not remarkably wide, and Canada is *right there*. It's another country but not another world, and it all looks the same from the shore except that the bridge overhead is far more impressive than any municipal river crossing would ever be anywhere else.

The rain is heavier now, streams of water running in rivulets toward downtown gutters and drains, diverted into the St. Clair, and ultimately bound for Detroit just like we are. But not before we wait out the coming cloudburst with coffee and soup in downtown Port Huron. The shower won't be over by the time we're done, but it will be lessened, and that's all we can really hope for.

The rain is subsided by the time we arrive in town of St. Clair, nearer than ever to the end of our adventure, but maybe the closest we'll ever be to the place where Michigan's story begins.

Before the state had borders, and before Detroit was a name worth knowing, there was St. Clair. It's the oldest named town in the state, and it's got the scars to prove it. Settlers, soldiers, and workers built it up along the river, and the river shaped everything that followed.

It started with the French. In 1679, Robert de La Salle and Father Louis Hennepin cruised through these waters, slapping the name Lac Sainte-Claire on the place after Saint Clare of Assisi, the patron saint of sore eyes and television (not that that last part made much sense at the time). The British came next, twisting it into St. Clair, and by 1764, settlers had carved out a foothold along the river. From that point on, St. Clair wasn't just a town. It was a waypoint, a trade hub, and a place that people either passed through or put down roots in for good.

As you might expect, the St. Clair River forms the spine and lifeblood of the town. St. Clair's boardwalk lines the shore of the river to create the longest freshwater boardwalk on the planet, but where you might expect a touristy carnival strip, instead it's a working-class promenade where the freighters pass so close you can feel the engine hum in your bones.

You would expect St. Clair to be involved in shipbuilding, and it absolutely was. But you might be surprised at the role the town has played in one of Michigan's quietest important industries: salt mining. The Diamond Crystal Salt Company, established in the late 19th century, helped turn Michigan into a major player in salt production. Beneath the soil, vast underground salt deposits stretched for miles, and St. Clair became one of the hubs for mining and refining this critical resource.

The salt industry wasn't glamorous, but it was essential. Michigan's salt deposits fueled industries from food preservation to chemical production, and St. Clair's workers toiled underground to extract the mineral that built businesses across the state. The salt was there before Henry Ford ever dreamed about cars, and it has lasted for more than a century beyond the deforestation of the state's timber. There's a certain irony in the fact that Michigan, best known for its abundance of fresh water, sits atop a wealth of salt.

But then, maybe it's fitting. After all, Michiganders have always been a little salty themselves. Hardworking, no-nonsense, and tough as nails, they built industries that shaped the nation, and they did it with grit and determination. The salt beneath their feet? Just another reminder that this place was never about glamour. It was about getting the job done.

Our penultimate ride ends in Marine City, and the town's name is an appropriate one. In the 1880s, its shipbuilders produced more wooden steamships than almost anywhere else, despite the fact that Marine City was never a large town and has never eclipsed more than 5,000 in population.

The town tells stories through its water. The St. Clair picks up speed at Marine City, its current strong enough to convey enormous ships even with their engines turned off. Beneath the waters, the river is so clear that historic shipwrecks are visible even from the shore. Right up until 2021, the builder's model of the Titanic had its home right here in Marine City. The incredibly detailed 1:48 scale model included more than 3,000,000 rivets and took longer to build than the actual Titanic itself. The model has since moved to Pennsylvania.

At Marine City, we settled into a cozy hotel room, washed the grit from our bodies, and spat it from our mouths. We ordered Detroit-style pizza and wandered the sidewalks through intermittent drizzle. We sidled up to the bar before an early night's sleep and I ordered an Old Fashioned.

"You want it Michigan style?" the bartender asked.

"What's that?"

"Only one way to find out."

I watched the bartender select a large ice cube with a pair of tongs, watched her slice a narrow section of orange peel, watched her pull a bright red cherry from a jar. I saw her mix the simple syrup with the Wild Turkey, heard the sound of the concoction being shaken. I watched the ice cube go into a glass that seemed like it was probably too big for the drink I had ordered, watched as she strained the contents of the shaker over the ice cube and into the glass. I watched as she expressed the oils of the orange peel and dropped the cherry in with a satisfying plunk.

And then, I watched with a slow creeping horror as she reached beneath the counter and produced a soda gun. She finished the drink off with Sprite, and it was a lot of Sprite.

When in Rome.

Bottoms up.

CHAPTER TWENTY-SIX
DETROIT

Marine City isn't exactly a metropolis, and it's still too far away from Detroit to be a suburb. But there's a different feeling when we ride off to begin our morning. The quiet lake towns of the north have ended, and for the rest of the way, we're pointed toward the churn of a city and an industrial din that is growing by degrees. There is less space now between the towns, less quiet on the roads, and less of the natural world all around us. Those things have been replaced in turn by sprawl, traffic, and infrastructure.

But today it's a Saturday morning and we've pushed off some hours after the fishermen and well before the sleepers-in. For at least an hour or two, we can still pretend we're further away from the end than we really are.

It's not eight miles and fewer than 30 minutes before we arrive in our first new town. This one is Algonac, and it's the place that took Detroit's obsession with automotive performance and made the obvious decision to put it on the water.

Let's start with Christopher Columbus Smith, because if you're named after one of history's most famous explorers, you'd better do something impressive. Smith did. In the early 1900s, he began building wooden boats in Algonac that would become the stuff of legend. He crafted weapons for the water, lean and mean, capable of speeds that left other boats in their wake, coughing up river water and defeat.

His company, Chris-Craft, became synonymous with speed, luxury, and American ingenuity. The boats were sleek, fast, and beautiful. Soon enough, they were attracting the kind of people who wanted all three – bootleggers, rich businessmen, and thrill-seekers who thought of the water as something to be conquered. Even the U.S. military took notice, eventually commissioning Chris-Craft boats for World War II. But before that, there was a man who would push Smith's designs even further, breaking records and egos along the way.

If Chris Smith gave Algonac speedboats, then it was Gar Wood who turned them into legends. This guy wasn't just a skilled boat-builder. He was a mad scientist of horsepower, the kind of man who looked at the water and thought, "What if I went so fast it caught fire?"

Wood took Chris-Craft's sleek designs and pushed them to their absolute limit. He built and piloted Miss America IX, the first boat to break 100 mph on water back in 1931 when most people still thought riding a bicycle downhill was risky. He won the Harmsworth Trophy again and again, embarrassing the British aristocracy, who thought they owned the concept of speed.

But Wood wasn't just about breaking records—his boats became the preferred getaway vehicles of the most daring rum-runners, the bootlegging kings who made Algonac's night-time river traffic look like a high-speed Hollywood car chase.

Picture this: It's 1926, a moonless night on the St. Clair River. The Canadian shore is barely a mile away, and just beneath the black water sits a fortune in barrels of whiskey waiting to be picked up. A crew of bootleggers, bundled up against the cold, loads case after case of Canadian Club and Seagram's into the belly of a waiting Gar Wood speedboat.

They know the risks. If the Coast Guard or federal agents catch them, it's prison or worse. But with a 500-horsepower Packard engine under the hood, they also know they've got the fastest damn boat on the water.

With a roar, the engine comes to life. The throttle is thrown forward. The boat lurches out of the darkness, slicing through the waves at 60, maybe 70 miles per hour. The wake boils behind them, and in minutes, they're across the river.

By the time the Coast Guard hears them, it's too late. Even if the agents get their own patrol boats fired up, they don't stand a chance. A Wood-designed hull is lighter, faster, and built to skim over the water like a skipping stone. The only thing the lawmen catch is a face full of spray and the sound of laughter disappearing into the night.

Did Gar Wood *know* that bootleggers were using his boats? Of course he did. How could he not?

But officially, he was just a businessman and a speed freak. His job was to build the fastest, sleekest boats in the world, not ask what people did with them. As long as the money was green, he didn't seem too interested in where it came from.

For more than a decade, Algonac's river traffic looked like a high-speed Hollywood chase, only with wooden speedboats, gun-toting agents, and barrels of booze. And every time a boat vanished into the mist, it was proof that Gar Wood had won again.

Algonac was a bootlegger's paradise, what with its proximity to Canada and its every growing supply of the fastest boats on the planet. But that wasn't all. Algonac sits at the mouth of the St. Clair Flats, a watery maze of channels and islands that form the largest freshwater delta in the world. Think of it like the Everglades but with worse weather and fewer gators. During Prohibition, these channels were a smuggler's dream; twisting, turning, and impossible to track unless you knew them by heart. Even if the feds could catch you out on the water, a skilled boatsmen could lead them directly into a labyrinth of marshy channels and then speed away down the other side. That meant that from 1920 to 1933, the St. Clair River was one of the busiest illegal liquor highways in America.

Of course, Algonac had a long history of filling the glasses at the local bar. Before there were rumrunners, there were ice harvesters, and there was probably some overlap between those two groups. Their jobs had a lot in common. They were out on the water, the work was dangerous, and the pay was generous – if you could live to receive it.

In the 1800s and early 1900s, before electric refrigeration, people needed ice to keep their food from rotting. And in the dead of winter, when the St. Clair River froze solid, the men of Algonac would carve the river into chunks the size of small boulders.

They used giant saws, horses, and pure brute force to drag the massive ice blocks onto waiting trains, which then hauled them all across the country. The work was brutal – frozen hands, busted limbs, and the ever-present danger of falling into the river and disappearing forever. But it paid, and in the days before bootlegging, it was one of the only games in town.

By the early 1900s, there was a lot going on in the river that people didn't know about, and it was more than just rumrunners. There are mysteries underneath the water too. Somewhere out there, beneath the St. Clair, you'll find the lost *City of Dresden*.

The *City of Dresden* was a massive steel hulled ship with an epic name, and no one knows why it sank beneath the waters. Some say structural failure, others say sabotage, and others still blame the rumrunners. The case has never been solved, and a hundred years later, divers are still looking for clues.

We push on, rolling toward the big city as the heat of the day begins to close in around us. People are awake now and people are in their cars and we are sharing their roads. Most of them seem okay with it. A few aren't. They make sure to let us know.

At Algonac, the St. Clair bends to the west and spills into Anchor Bay. We follow the water to the west and then to the north. For a time the tailwinds become headwinds, at least until we arrive in New Baltimore and point our bikes southward for the last time.

Before it was a lakeside city known for summer tourism and waterfront charm, New Baltimore was nothing more than dense woods, open water, and the quiet movements of the indigenous tribes who lived there for centuries. That all changed when a man named Pierre Yax arrived in 1796, setting the stage for what would become one of Michigan's oldest continually inhabited waterfront settlements.

Pierre Yax was no stranger to the frontier. He was born in Grosse Pointe, New France (now Michigan) when it was still a French-controlled fur trading post. By the late 18th century, as the British and Americans jockeyed for control over the Great Lakes, Yax took a gamble and ventured into what was then virtually uncharted land on the shores of Anchor Bay, part of Lake St. Clair.

At a time when Michigan was still a wilderness dominated by indigenous people, fur trappers, and the occasional military outpost, Yax staked his claim. In 1826, he formalized his hold on the land with a land grant signed by President John Quincy Adams, cementing his role as the founding settler of New Baltimore.

Fast forward to 1845, and the settlement that Pierre Yax started was still just a collection of farms and homesteads. That's when Alfred Ashley, a businessman from Mount Clemens, decided the spot had potential for something much bigger. He saw waterfront commerce, industry, and growth.

Ashley purchased 60 acres of land along both sides of Washington Street, laying out the town's first official plat. He didn't just claim the land. He put it to work. He built the first sawmill, a dock, and set the foundations for an actual economy. No longer just a backwoods settlement, Ashley's vision made it a town.

To make it official, a post office was established in 1851 under the name "Ashleyville." This might have been the name we used today, except the locals had other plans.

By 1867, the community had grown large enough to justify official incorporation, and it needed a name that fit its rising stature. Rather than stick with Ashleyville, residents opted for New Baltimore, likely inspired by the original Baltimore, a city with a similar waterfront character and a strong shipping industry.

Depending on who you ask, New Baltimore is either the furthest flung of Detroit's many moons, or the last independent town before you enter the Motor City's orbit. Either way, the city is looming, and the city is coming soon. But before we can get there, we will have to endure just one more suburb.

*   *   *

There is a lot of money that has left Detroit during the past century, but a bike ride through Grosse Pointe is enough to persuade you that the wealth hasn't gone very far.

Grosse Pointe isn't just rich. It's obscene. It's the kind of wealth that doesn't need to prove itself. It already did, a hundred years ago. While other Detroit suburbs were built by people chasing the American Dream, Grosse Pointe was built by people who had already won it and were now just showing off.

This isn't new money. This is old money, the kind that doesn't shout. It whispers, because it doesn't need to explain itself. Grosse Pointe was where Detroit's industrial elite retreated when they wanted the perks of high society without having to see the factories that paid for it all.

Most suburbs have nice houses. Grosse Pointe has estates. The kinds with gates, chauffeurs, and rooms people haven't stepped foot in for a decade. The kinds where the front door is just for show because the servants use the side entrance.

We're talking French chateaus, Italian palazzos, and Tudor-style castles, all plopped along the shores of Lake St. Clair, because if you're going to be rich, you might as well have a view to go with it. The ride along Lakeshore Drive is a real estate flex of ridiculous proportions – mile after mile of mansions so massive, they look like something out of a Gatsby fever dream.

These weren't built by some guy who got lucky in the stock market last week. These were built by the Fords, Dodges, Fishers, and other auto barons; the people who created the modern world and then built houses massive enough to remind everyone of it.

Grosse Pointe isn't just about what you own. It's about where you belong. And if you don't belong, you stay out. The clubs here aren't just expensive. They are exclusive in a way that money alone can't buy you into.

The Grosse Pointe Yacht Club? Not just a yacht club. It's a floating fortress of prestige, with a marina that looks more like a private navy than a collection of boats.

The Country Club of Detroit? One of the oldest in the country. Founded in 1897, it has hosted the kinds of golf matches where the losers still leave in Bentleys.

And then there's The Little Club, where if you have to ask how to get in, you won't.

The thing about Grosse Pointe wealth is that it isn't flashy. It's refined. The rich here don't need gold-plated Lamborghinis or diamond-studded watches. They have art collections worth more than small countries, private foundations that control billions, and family legacies that span generations.

It's not about what you buy, it's about what you inherit. And in Grosse Pointe, you don't just inherit money, you inherit power, prestige, and the expectation that you will carry it well.

And for the people who live here, the ones who have everything whenever they want it, there's an ever-present reminder that somehow manages to keep them humble. There's one estate that rises above the rest, a whisper to the millionaires that no matter how wealthy you are...

...you're still not the Ford family.

If Henry Ford was the king of industry, then his son, Edsel Ford, was the prince of style. And nowhere is that more obvious than in the house he built in Grosse Pointe Shores, a sprawling, 60-room English-style manor that oozes old money sophistication. This wasn't just a home. It was a statement of wealth, taste, and the kind of quiet power that doesn't need to scream to be heard.

While his father, Henry, built his mansion, Fair Lane, like an industrial fortress, Edsel had a different idea of what luxury should look like. Where Henry was about function, Edsel was about beauty. The Edsel & Eleanor Ford House is proof of what happens when someone with unlimited money and an impeccable sense of style decides to build the perfect home. The place is 30,000 square feet, has 60 rooms, and 87 acres of waterfront property on Lake St. Clair.

It comes with gardens that make Versailles look modest, and it's got it's own lagoon, because of course it does.

Designed by renowned architect Albert Kahn, the estate was built in 1928, at a time when the rest of America was about to eat dirt in the Great Depression. But in Grosse Pointe, the money never stops moving.

Most rich people slap together a mansion with whatever is trending at the time. Not Edsel. He wanted something timeless. Something elegant. Something that looked like it had been there for centuries, even though it was brand new.

So he imported entire stone facades from English manors to make sure the place had the kind of weathered, old-world charm that money can't usually buy. The result? A perfect Tudor-revival mansion that looks like it was ripped straight out of the English countryside and dropped onto Detroit's wealthiest shoreline.

Inside, it's just as jaw-dropping, with hand-carved wood paneling from actual English estates, custom-designed stained-glass windows that make churches jealous, a grand staircase that looks like royalty should be descending it at all times. Each of its rooms were basically miniature art galleries, filled with pieces from Van Gogh, Cézanne, and Diego Rivera.

Edsel Ford died in 1943, and his widow, Eleanor, lived in the home until 1976. Her will gave the estate to the public, and today the Grosse Pointe Ford home stands as a museum and as one of the finest historic houses in America.

The rest of Grosse Pointe has been aspiring to reach the heights of the Edsel Ford Home ever since. Mansions with audacious gables soar toward the sky, lakefront views are planned and sculpted, their brick fences and gates alone costing more than my house. The streets are cleaned immaculately, and I am sure I see artistic detail works stenciled into the sewer grates. Somehow, everyone's car is clean all of the time. The gas station on the corner is built with marled brick and dressed up like a glitzy suburban library. We round one corner and then another; impressive mansions, blue horizons, gorgeous trees perfectly pruned.

And then, in a shocking and sudden instant, Detroit is there to punch us in the mouth.

There is no transition between Grosse Pointe and Detroit. There is no margin between the municipalities, no fading gradient where one place blends into the other. It just happens, and when it happens, you don't need anyone to tell you that it did. There's a *Welcome to Detroit* sign at the city's limits. They should have spent their money on something else. Believe me, you already know.

In a span of less than 20 feet, everything changes. The buildings here have holes where the windows used to be. There are loose bricks in the street and shattered glass on the sidewalk. We ride past a burned out car and an abandoned city bus. There is an overturned port-a-potty in the bike lane, and the overturned port-a-potty is leaking. If we stopped right now and looked behind us, we would see all of it – the car, the toilet, the decay – and we would still see the opulence of Grosse Pointe barely a quarter mile away.

But we don't stop. We don't dare stop. This is the part of Detroit where whatever you do, you keep going. We pedal through the Detroit they warned you about wondering how long it will be until we're back into the Detroit we loved. The Detroit they warned you about lasts for a long time. The St. Clair River has become Lake St. Clair, and by the time we reach Belle Isle, Lake St. Clair has narrowed itself into the Detroit River.

We're closer to the end now, scooting onto Detroit's crowded riverwalk, skateboarding our bikes through crowds of families trying to enjoy a summer day on the narrow strip of Detroit that's still beautiful and worth seeing. It's a harrowing finish down a road that looks like it's under construction, but actually that's just the way the road is now. And then we're back at Riverside Park, the place where it all started for us, and the end of one hell of a ride. My friend Jared is waiting there for us with his van, and he asks us what we're wanting for. It's a tough question to answer.

I want another South Haven sunset, another slice of Detroit style pizza, I want a Gatorade and I want a shower. I want ice cream from Bay City and I want cheese from a cave near Suttons Bay. I want to see just one more lighthouse. Maybe two. I want to have the time to see more of the mansions we had to ride past, and I want to survey a hundred haunted shipwrecks from the safety of a glass-bottomed boat. I want to get out of these bike shorts. I want a Belgian beer from Frankfort and then I want another one. I want chocolate covered cherries from Traverse City, and I want to sit on the beach at St. Joseph. I want to see the amazing towns we never got to see just because they weren't on the shore: Kalamazoo, Grand Rapids, Lansing, Ann Arbor, Saginaw, Cadillac, and of course, Hell. I want some ibuprofen. I want to take my time at the scenic outlooks we had to race through during the days before. I want to go back to the Tunnel of Trees. I want to try the fudge. I want a baked potato wrapped in a pizza. I want to sleep in my own bed. I want to pause longer at the most incredible bridges I've ever seen. I want a Vernor's. I want to settle this Paul Bunyan thing once and for all. I want to see the museums we had to skip. I want a massage. I want to stop at the Saugatuck art shoppes again. I want to drink early morning coffee beneath a pine tree stand and watch the sunrise through the steam over my mug. I want to start all over again, because Michigan is an adventure that's always changing. I want to sit and rest for a while because the tourists don't have it all wrong. I want to buy a cutting board in the shape of Michigan's lower peninsula. I want to kiss my wife because I can't believe she let me talk her into this. I want to listen to Lose Yourself. I want to see the Van Goghs. I want to apologize to Detroit for the way we have – all of us – taken it for granted. I want to sift for lost cities in the sand. I want to find a Petoskey stone. I want to spark an uprising designed to bring Toledo back to Michigan. I want to watch a Tigers game in the sunshine. I want someone to make me an Old Fashioned, and I don't want any Sprite in it.

ABOUT THE AUTHOR

Aaron Helman is an adventurer, historian, humorist, and author. He is the author of <u>An Incomplete History of St. Joseph County, Indiana</u>, <u>Ride the Jack Rabbit</u>, and <u>On the Southernmost Bend</u>.

Learn more about Aaron's books, events, and upcoming projects at aaronhelman.com.

Reach out anytime to aaron.helman@gmail.com.